Shotgun Marksmanship

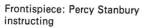

Frontispiece: Percy Stanbury
instructing

Shotgun Marksmanship

Percy Stanbury and G. L. Carlisle

Photography by G. L. Carlisle

Fourth Edition

Stanley Paul

London   Melbourne   Auckland   Johannesburg

Stanley Paul & Co. Ltd

An imprint of Century Hutchinson Ltd

Brookmount House, 62-65 Chandos Place,
Covent Garden, London WC2N 4NW

Century Hutchinson Publishing Group (Australia) Pty Ltd
16-22 Church Street, Hawthorn, Melbourne, Victoria 3122

Century Hutchinson Group (NZ) Ltd
32-34 View Road, PO Box 40-086, Glenfield, Auckland 10

Century Hutchinson Group (SA) (Pty) Ltd
PO Box 337, Bergvlei 2012, South Africa

First published by Herbert Jenkins 1962
Reprinted 1963 and 1965
Second edition published by Barrie & Jenkins 1969
Reprinted 1971
Third edition 1974
Reprinted 1977
Fourth edition 1980
Reprinted by Stanley Paul 1985, 1986

© Percy Stanbury and G. L. Carlisle 1962, 1969, 1974 and 1980

Set in Monotype Times New Roman

Printed and bound in Great Britain by
Anchor Brendon Ltd, Tiptree, Essex

British Library Cataloguing in Publication Data
Stanbury, Percy
  Shotgun marksmanship. – 4th ed.
  1. Fowling
  I. Title II. Carlisle, Gordon Lowther
  799.2′4   SK311
ISBN 0 09 142360 0

Contents

Appendices

Foreword by the Earl of Northesk

It is a great honour to have been asked to write a short Foreword to this book and I do so with pleasure as a tribute to Percy Stanbury, to whom what success and the great enjoyment I have had shooting are entirely due.

G. L. Carlisle brings to the book, through his varied shooting experience, the outlook of the 'average' shot, while Stanbury's skill as a game shot, his wonderful performances with clay pigeon and his expert handling of a rifle, coupled with a charming personality and great patience, have placed him at the top of his profession as a coach.

There can be few, if any, who take up shooting under his tuition who do not develop into a reasonable, and most important, a safe shot; while the good shot who has temporarily 'gone off' will have the fault quickly pointed out and after a short practice be back on form again with regained confidence.

Most of the secrets of his success as a coach are clearly and simply explained in the book which will, I am sure, be welcomed by the beginner, the average shot and the expert alike. The beginner would do well to read this book before even having his or her first lesson and again to read the relevant chapter or chapters after each lesson.

The book covers every aspect of game shooting, and particularly interesting is the diagram and explanation of the working of the Safety Catch – a part of the gun not always fully understood by many shooting men.

I cannot wait to add this book to my library, as reading it once rather hurriedly, has given me the appetite to read and re-read it again.

NORTHESK

Bear Farm, Binfield
Bracknell, Berkshire

Preface

This book describes how to shoot straight. It deals with shotguns and their cartridges, how a gun should be fitted to its user and how he should control it in a manner which will enable him to hit his target. It is a treatise on 'how to hit what you aim at'.

The gun as a weapon is printed with a small 'g'. The Gun as the man who wields that weapon is printed with a capital 'G'.

The reader is advised to look at the illustrations first before reading the book. He will then gain an understanding of the method of straight shooting advocated in the text.

The authors wish to express their thanks to those kind friends who allowed themselves to be photographed to demonstrate good style, and bad.

Illustrations

Photographs

Figures

NOTE: Similar photographs to those illustrating wrong positions may often be seen in papers and magazines which publish articles on shooting. Sometimes the pictures are captioned, 'Mr X shooting woodcock', or, 'Mr Y takes a high pheasant.' After studying this book it may be that the reader will examine such shooting pictures with a more knowledgeable eye, and will feel entitled to murmur to himself, 'More likely, "Mr X shooting *at* woodcock" and "Mr Y *missing* a high pheasant."'

1 Guns

Game guns are made in a greater variety of details than even many experienced shots realize. Certainly the newcomer to shooting, and indeed anyone contemplating buying a gun, should consider carefully some of the many factors which can influence the choice of the most suitable gun for the individual.

The first decision to be made when buying a gun concerns the main purpose for which it is to be used. Probably the most widely used general game gun is the 12-bore with 28-inch barrels and chambered for $2\frac{1}{2}$-inch cartridges, weighing about $6\frac{1}{2}$lb. But a different bore, or barrel length or chamber, or weight may be more suitable for the needs of any particular shooter. Wildfowling guns, pigeon guns, clay shooting guns all have detailed differences for their especial purpose. The physical build of the shooter also affects his choice of gun, and, of course, so does his financial position.

Usually, a heavy gun is a steady one so that 7 lb. is not too much for the average man to wield although lighter and, therefore, short-barrelled weapons may be preferred by small men and for short-range driven birds such as partridges. The average man of about 5 ft 10 in. is generally suited by a 28-inch 12-bore and the 6 ft fellow with a long reach can well take 30-inch barrels. Long barrels reduce muzzle blast and recoil and help towards steady shooting.

The term 'bore' to indicate calibre is very old and is based on the diameter of lead balls: if 12 balls the same diameter as a gun barrel weigh 1 lb. that barrel is termed '12-bore'. Lead balls to fit a 16-bore run 16 to the pound, and for an 8-bore 8 to the pound, and so on. Smaller guns, 16, 20 and 28 bore, are suitable for ladies, boys or for older and less active men but it must be appreciated that variations in a gun's chamber, its choke and the load in the cartridges can affect its hitting power: bore alone is not a criterion of effectiveness. The larger bores, 10, 8 and 4, are used for wildfowling and particularly against geese. They are rarely seen nowadays, mostly because of the cost of the cartridges and the difficulty of obtaining them. The smallest shotgun in common use is measured not by 'bore' but in inches: it is the 'Four Ten', ·410 inch in diameter. In single barrel form with bolt action it is cheap, effective against rats, rabbits and squirrels and it is probably the ideal weapon for introducing the 12-year-old boy to shotgun shooting. But the 12-bore is the standard and most popular shotgun and for it have been developed many variations, which are considered below.

When buying a gun the services of a reputable dealer should be sought and, as with most things, quality pays; the best-quality guns are made in England. The term 'best gun' is used for top-quality guns and they, like Rolls Royce motor cars, are very expensive but are built with superb craftsmanship and will stand up to a lifetime of hard work. However, the sort of hard shooting that a best gun will accept is denied to most of us, anyway, and so this is a case when second best will do.

Most shooters who are limited in the price they can pay for a gun are best advised to decide very carefully what they want and then go out and search for it. A second-hand gun may well do but finding a gun with the right features of barrel length, choke, chamber, weight and so on may require much time and patience. If you buy a new gun should you take a ready-made one or have it made for you? Without a doubt, it *should* be made for you; it is more important to good shooting to have your gun made for you than your clothes. It is possible, however, to have new ready-made guns and old second-hand ones fitted to individual requirements, within reasonable limits. Fitting is vital: it is discussed in Chapter 3.

A shotgun barrel may be bored as a true cylinder throughout its length, or it may have the last couple of inches at its muzzle tapered so as to squeeze together the shot charge as it leaves the muzzle and so effect a denser pattern of pellets; the amount of tapering is called 'choke' and it may vary in reducing the diameter by only 3 thousandths of an inch to as much as 40 thousandths. The usual chokes found on most guns are 'improved cylinder', 'half choke' and 'full choke', but it should be noted that the term 'choke' engraved on the flats of the barrels of a gun does not necessarily mean full choke; it gives no indication of how *much* choke a barrel has and the only way to find out this in the case of a second-hand gun is to have it measured by a gunsmith. Shot pattern cannot be at its best at all ranges and a gun that is choked so as to be effective at long range (40–50 yards) will throw a tight pattern at short range (15–20 yards) which will either miss the target or pulverize it; similarly, a lightly choked barrel producing a good pattern for driven partridges at perhaps 20 yards will not be very effective at high pheasants. Most game guns therefore, have a lightly choked right barrel, probably improved cylinder, and a more heavily choked left barrel, probably $\frac{1}{2}$ or $\frac{3}{4}$ choke. The effect on the shot pattern of varying degrees of choke is shown in Table 5.

Working our way down the gun, the next item to consider is the rib, that strip of metal between and on top of the two barrels. Ribs may be smooth, and slightly U-shaped, or they may be raised and flat; they may also be file-cut or matted. Most inexpensive guns have smooth engine-turned ribs but their critics suggest that bright sunlight may glint on them and distract the shooter. Certainly, guns built primarily for clay-pigeon shooting usually have raised ribs with a matt surface. The choice is a matter of individual preference, and perhaps even idiosyncrasy. Some guns, particularly those used for trap shooting, have ventilated ribs, whose advantage is somewhat doubtful; probably their popularity is due to good salesmanship! In fact, the barrels and ribs are scarcely seen at all by the man behind the gun whose eye must always be on the target; still less does he see the bead or foresight, usually placed at the muzzle of a shotgun, except possibly when taking a sitting shot. Wildfowlers, however, have been known to enlarge this bead with a blob of mud in order to help them know where the ends of their barrels are when swinging onto a duck in the dark.

12-bores may be chambered to take cartridges of 2, $2\frac{1}{2}$, $2\frac{3}{4}$ or 3 inches, $2\frac{1}{2}$ being the standard. Killing power will vary according to the shot load used and, while the 2-inch cartridge virtually reduces the effect of a gun to that of a 16 or 20 bore, the bigger cartridge enables it to compete with larger bored guns. The 3-inch 12-bore, called a 'magnum', is an excellent goose gun, its ammunition is cheaper and more easily obtainable than that of an 8-bore and, although it probably weighs about $7\frac{1}{2}$ lb., it can be used with a $2\frac{1}{2}$-inch cartridge for normal game shooting. The $2\frac{3}{4}$-inch chambered gun, at about 7 lb., is a compromise for the man who wishes to combine a game gun and a wildfowling gun. Shot loads are discussed in Chapter 2.

Provision must be made on any gun for the removal of fired cartridges and on cheap guns this is achieved by the extractors at the breech pushing the cartridges back half an inch when the gun is opened; the cartridges must then be pulled out by hand. Such a gun is called a 'non ejector'. An 'ejector' gun, not normally called an automatic ejector since the 'automatic' part is taken for granted, has a spring in the fore-end which strikes the extractors sharply so that the cartridges fly out of the breech as soon as the gun is opened. An ejector is preferable for nearly all types of shooting, although there are wildfowlers who claim that a non-ejector is preferable on the shore since there are less working parts liable to become clogged with mud.

The lock is the heart of a gun, controlling the actual firing of it. Box locks, or 'Anson and Deeley type', are strong, simple and adequate but more expensive guns nearly always have side locks. The advantage of the side lock is that its longer spring permits of finer adjustment of trigger pressure so that it could safely be adjusted to a light pressure of about $2\frac{1}{2}$ lb. if required; also, the pull on the trigger will be sweeter than with a box lock. Side locks look attractive and enhance the beauty of the gun.

Triggers should fit conveniently to the finger and the pull should be steady and crisp. The pull needed to trip the sear ought to be about 4 lb. and adjustment is necessary if the pull is more than about a pound either side of this. Some guns have only a single trigger which operates each barrel in turn; this is satisfactory provided a choice of barrels can be made, otherwise the single trigger can be a considerable nuisance to a shooter who wants to fire his choked left barrel at a distant target but is unable to do so until he has emptied his right unchoked barrel. A single trigger is easier to operate than two when wearing gloves.

Although the hammerless ejector is the most popular type of gun, non-ejectors can be quite satisfactory and so can hammer guns: both characteristics make for cheapness. The vitally important thing about a hammer gun is that its owner should be especially careful about safety; the sight of a cocked hammer gun over its owner's arm while the barrels point at his friends' feet or their dogs as the Guns stand around in a circle, chatting, is enough to make any sensible man run for cover. New hammer guns are made, mostly outside England, but the majority of them seen in the field are old guns whose hammers, one feels, might fly off at any moment. Strictly speaking, hardly anyone should ever see such a

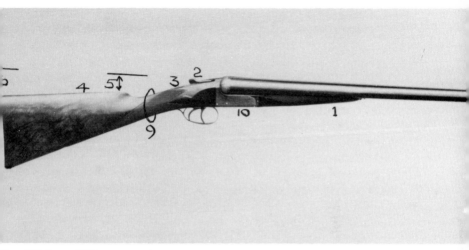

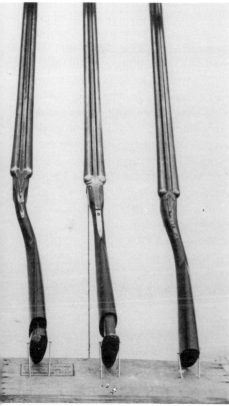

1 *Above* **The parts of a gun** 1 Fore-end. 2. Top lever. 3 Safety catch. 4 Comb. 5 Bend, or drop, at comb. 6 Bend, or drop, at heel. 7 Heel, or bump, of butt. 8 Toe of butt. 9 Small of the butt, or grip, or hand. 10 Lock. Note that the ends of the muzzles are not shown

2 *Below* **Try-guns** On the left is a try-gun with an across-eyed stock. In the centre is a try-gun set with a good deal of cast-off; the vertical black line indicates how the stock has been moved to the right of the line of the barrels. On the right is a gun with considerable cast-off to place the barrels between the shooter's eyes, when neither eye is the master; this is a central-vision stock. Ends of muzzles not shown

gun cocked, since the correct way to use it in company is always to have it uncocked, even when walking-up. The right thumb can rest lightly on the hammers and as the gun is thrown up so the thumb flicks back the hammers, just as with a hammerless gun the thumb pushes forward the safety catch, in the moment before the butt reaches the shoulder.

In the stock of a gun is the secret of its fit. Even the stock of a second-hand gun may be bent to fit its new owner and it can also be lengthened or cut down. Walnut is used almost exclusively, plain straight-grained wood from the trunk of the tree for cheaper guns and beautiful mottled wood from the roots for expensive guns. The better-quality wood is, incidentally, easier to bend to the precise requirements of a customer. The grip for the right hand is usually straight and this is certainly better for use with two triggers since the hand can slide back more easily to enable the forefinger to reach correctly on to the left trigger. Half-pistol grips are common on continental guns but their real use should be only for single-trigger guns. Full-pistol grips are occasionally found but they are not suitable for the normal user; they can be a help when there is some deformity of the hand. A recoil pad on the butt is generally something of a fad: it should not be necessary on a properly balanced and fitted gun. There can be a tendency for the rubber of a recoil pad to stick on the shooter's clothing and check the movement of the butt into the shoulder. If a pad is used it must be top quality and should preferably be leather-covered to prevent the rubber entangling with the clothing.

Automatics and over-and-under guns are not normally reckoned as standard game guns although they do have their devotees, more particularly for clay shooting. They tend to be heavier than side-by-side double barrelled guns, and automatics, even when in fairness only loaded with two cartridges, are somewhat distrusted by standard gun users: one of the reasons is that an automatic cannot be broken so that all the world can see that it is unloaded and safe. The single barrel 12-bore is considerably cheaper than the double and it may well be a good buy for a young man who is unable to pay much for his weapon; it might even encourage him to concentrate on accuracy with his one barrel and not just to shoot off quickly, reckoning that there is a second barrel to follow if he

3 **A security gun cabinet**   Steel, with special locks. It should be bolted to the wall

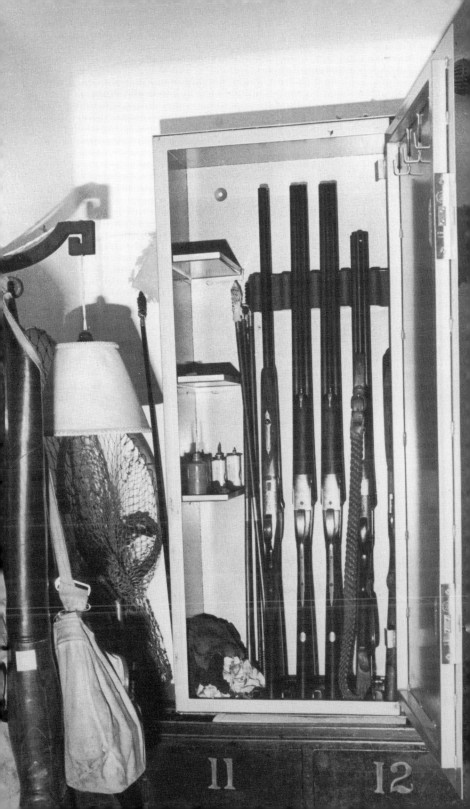

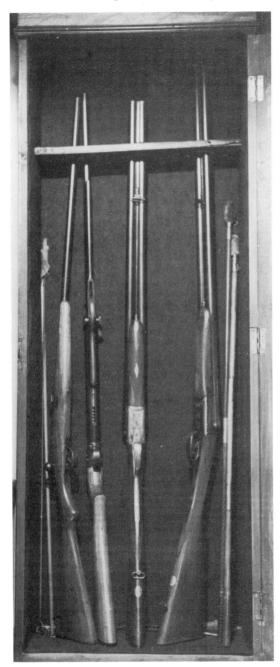

4 The gun cupboard
A small glass-fronted
gun cupboard to delight
the owner's eye. The
modest armoury
consists of: ·410, ·22 air
rifle, 12-bore game gun,
12-bore magnum. Both
12-bores are fitted with
sling swivels

misses with the first. Incidentally, there are purists who maintain that the object of the second barrel is to hit another bird, not to have a second go at one missed with the first barrel, and that to use the second barrel in that way is unsporting.

Among gun accessories one of the most useful is a sling which is easily fitted with small mountings beneath the barrels and near the toe of the butt. For rough shooting, pigeon shooting and wildfowling a sling is invaluable as it allows both hands to be free when carrying a hide and decoys, when jumping ditches, and on the long plod back in the dark carrying, we hope, a handful of duck. For shooting in more select company the sling is easily removed. Nearly everyone who has once seen a sling in use agrees on its advantages, but remarkably few bother to fit one; sling users wonder why.

Every gun should have a gun case, an oblong flat box in which the dismantled gun may be packed, but it should also have a cover or slip; made of canvas or leather, this takes the assembled gun and protects it while travelling by car to and from the shoot or even between drives. The gun owner who enjoys his weapons may sooner or later also acquire a gun cupboard through whose glass front he may look and admire. . . . A battery of guns always looks good to the enthusiast but even just one or two in a cupboard can bring joy to the eye of the beholder. A gun, like a car or a camera or a watch, can be a beautiful thing and standing upright in its cupboard it is shown to its advantage and, moreover, it is easily available to be taken out and inspected and perhaps offered for admiration by its proud owner to an interested friend. Below the gun cupboard, of course, should be a smaller cupboard with solid door and shelves, or perhaps drawers, in which are kept the cleaning materials.

Unfortunately, thefts of guns have increased recently, and the ordinary householder is advised not to keep his weapons where they may easily be found by an intruder. Glass-fronted cupboards are better replaced by security cabinets of steel with special locks; in their absence, guns should be kept out of sight, and removal of the fore-end will render them inoperative. But it won't necessarily stop them being stolen! Cartridges should not be stored in the same place, less to deter thieves than to lessen the risk of children loading a gun.

Gun cleaning has become much simpler in recent years since the introduction of cartridges with non-corrosive primers and impreg-

5 Gun cleaning   Gun cleaning at the end of the day. Instruction for
boys, usually very keen to learn the correct drill

nated wads which partially clean the weapon each time it is fired.
Nonetheless a few hints may be worth while:

1   Have two cleaning rods, one for the cleaning rag or brush and
    one for the oily mop used for finally oiling the barrels after
    cleaning.
2   Push small bits of rolled-up newspaper through the barrels in
    the first place thus removing the main dirt and prolonging the
    life of the cleaning rag.
3   Instead of using ordinary rag or tow for cleaning the barrels
    try the special Shotgun Patches made by Parker Hale; these
    are made the right size according to bore and so save time.

4 Have a phosphor-bronze brush for stubborn bits of fouling.
5 Use a rust-preventing oil, such as 'Young's ·303 cleaner, and
  a lighter oil, like Three-in-One, for the working parts.
6 Use a feather, the quill for cleaning round and under the extractors and the soft end for lightly oiling the triggers, base
  of the rib, etc. A fairly stiff feather such as that from a pigeon's
  tail is better than a soft one like a pheasant's.
7 If the gun is very wet after rain stand it on its muzzles to drain
  the water away down the barrels and not back into the action.
  Use blotting paper for drying such places as the base of the rib
  where it joins the barrels. Examine the gun the day after cleaning to see if there is any sweating, which will need wiping and
  re-oiling. After a wet day the locks of a side-lock gun can be
  removed, or the bottom plate of a box-lock, and water mopped
  out with a clean cotton rag. The screwdriver must fit the screw
  heads accurately, which probably means that it will need filing
  in order to enter the fine slots. Many gunsmiths, however,
  consider that unskilled owners would do less harm to their
  guns if they did *not* attempt to take them to bits!

A point about gun care on which there is both ignorance and
controversy concerns the release of the springs in the locks and the
ejector when the gun is put away after use. Most people like to
discharge the locks and some still maintain that this must be done;
if it is done the triggers must not be pulled without some resistance
being offered to the strikers, which otherwise may be broken. This
resistance may be provided by using snap-caps, which are like
metal cartridge cases with a sprung primer; they may be bought
at any gun shop. An alternative is to hold a coin against the striker,
after taking the barrels off the stock, and then pull the trigger.
Snap-caps have another use in that they enable the gun to be
fired when practising, as described in Chapter 10.

After a gun has been fired, either with real cartridges or snap-
caps and it is then opened to eject the cartridges, the fall of the
muzzles on opening re-cocks the lock hammers; if the fore-end is
then removed with the gun open, the snap-caps replaced in the
breech, gun closed and triggers pulled again, both main lock springs
and ejector springs will have been released. The barrels may then
be lifted off and the gun put away. Once the ejector springs have
been so released, however, it may be difficult to fit the fore-end on
again when putting the gun together. In this case the ejector kick-

ers must be cocked either by pressing them firmly and carefully against the edge of a wooden table or bench, or by pulling out the extractors, replacing the fore-end and then pressing the extractors back against the edge of the bench.

The controversial part of all this is that some experts tell us that it is unnecessary to let down the springs before putting a gun away, for steel does not acquire a permanent set nor lose its strength from being kept in a state of stress and in any case, the springs are only relieved to a very small extent. You cannot let down the sear springs of a gun, anyway, and the lock springs of very old guns still work so perhaps it is all rather a waste of time. Nevertheless, gun owners all have pet idiosyncracies and if you *want* to relieve the pressure on the lock and ejector springs you will not be doing any harm, it may make you feel better and at least you now know how to do it.

A final point of care concerns the stock. It should always be wiped clean of mud, and raw linseed oil rubbed well in is the best preservative. If you want to raise a bit more of a shine on the stock use 'artist's quality' linseed oil mixed with about a third as much turpentine. Do not smother the wood with gun oil which can cause it to swell and interfere with the working of the lock so that it becomes unsafe, as explained on page 152. Dents and scratches can be dealt with by applying wet felt and pressing on it with a hot iron: the steam forced into the wood raises the mark.

If you buy a second-hand gun you must, for your own safety, ensure that it has been submitted to the London or Birmingham Proof House for nitro-proofing. The pressure induced by a standard 12-bore cartridge with $1\frac{1}{16}$ oz. shot load is $2\frac{1}{2}$ tons per square inch at one inch from the breech, but a gun sent for Proof is submitted to pressures far greater than this. If it passes the test Proof marks are engraved on the flats of the barrels. An old and worn gun, even if it has once been proofed, may be out of proof so that a buyer is advised to send it to the Proof House for testing before paying for it; such action is, in fact, to the advantage of the dealer also since he is liable to prosecution if he sells a gun out of proof. The position is explained in 'Notes on the Proof of Shotguns and other Small Arms' issued by the Proof authorities and dated June 1960. Extracts are as follows:

The present law on the subject is to be found in the Gun Barrel Proof Acts of 1868 and 1950. . . .

The Proof Acts lay down that no small arm may be sold . . . unless and until it has been fully proved and duly marked. The maximum penalty for such offences is £20 per barrel.

Arms previously proved . . . are deemed unproved if the barrels have been enlarged in the bore beyond certain defined limits, or if the barrel or action has been materially weakened in other respect. . . .

The offence in dealing in unproved arms is committed by the seller, not by an unwitting purchaser.

Note that the Gun Barrel Proof Act 1978 increased the penalty above from £20 per barrel to £1000 for each offence.

As a final word on guns mention should be made of pair guns. These, as the name implies, are exactly matched pairs used for fast shooting with the assistance of a loader when driven game is presented in large numbers. Normally the guns are best guns and are made together and remain in the same ownership for years. Sometimes, however, pairs are split and sold separately and, as a corollary, a buyer may obtain a very good second-hand gun and subsequently, when opportunity of first class shooting occurs, he may wish to obtain a 'pair' to his one gun. Cases have occurred of advertisements in the sporting press resulting in a long separated pair being brought together again, but one good gun can usually be 'paired' to another if it is returned to its maker; he will probably be able to find another very similar gun and, by adapting it, make it pair up with his customer's one gun. Shooting with two guns is on the increase again and it is as well to know that matched guns can be obtained without the outlay of an excessive sum of money.

2 Cartridges

A cartridge is 'loaded' with powder and shot but the term 'load' is somewhat loosely used and it nearly always refers to the shot load only. Hand-loaded cartridges can be made to a customer's requirements but we shall consider here only factory-made cartridges as currently produced in Great Britain.

The largest firm of cartridge makers in this country use several different powders in their range of standard cartridges. But the customer need not be concerned with details of the powder as all he usually considers is the shot load (how many pellets), the shot size and the cartridge size: obviously a bigger cartridge will contain more powder and will have a longer range. For any particular powder the charge and wadding are so arranged as to give a standard mean velocity of about 1,070 feet per second over 20 yards. High velocity powders give a speed of about 1130 feet per second with a slightly longer range or, which may be more important, greater hitting power at a given range.

Standard shot loads for various bores and cartridge lengths are shown in Table 2, page 40. The popular load for a $2\frac{1}{2}$-inch case 12-bore for game shooting is $1\frac{1}{16}$ oz. and for trapshooting it is $1\frac{1}{8}$ oz.; lighter loads, e.g. 1 oz., are suitable for a shooter who suffers from gun headache if he fires many cartridges with a normal load; heavier-than-standard loads, for extra killing power, require longer cases, of $2\frac{3}{4}$ or 3 inches, or a bigger bore such as 10 or 8.

Shot sizes are lettered for the bigger sizes and numbered for the smaller ones, the numbers in ascending order indicating smaller pellets. Number 6 shot is probably the most commonly used in

---

6 **The eye above the barrels** A perfect position for the eye above barrels, neither too high nor too low. The eye is wholly visible above the rib, but no part of the cheek shows

Great Britain for normal game shooting. Other countries have different ways of designating their shot sizes and these are shown in Table 3, page 40.

The number of pellets in a cartridge depends on the shot load and the size of the shot: the bigger the pellets, which means that they are designated by a *smaller* number, the less of them there can be in the cartridge. The numbers of pellets in various game charges and for the more commonly used shot sizes are shown in Table 4, page 41.

The maximum killing range of a 12-bore game gun is generally reckoned to be 40 yards and at this range the spread of the shot pattern is considerable; from an improved cylinder barrel it is about 50 inches and even with full choke it is 40 inches, these figures being for the bulk of the charge and discounting stray pellets which may be well outside the pattern. But a 30-inch circle is the standard spread used in considering whether the number of pellets from a certain shot load and thrown by a specific boring is likely to result in a kill. So the next table we may consider shows the percentage of the total pellets of a charge which will be within the 30-inch circle at different ranges for various borings. Table 5 is on page 41.

From here we go to the actual number, not the percentage, of pellets in the 30-inch circle and this is given in Table 6 on page 42. This is confined to shot sizes 4, 5, 6 and 7 and for loads of $1\frac{1}{16}$ oz. and $1\frac{1}{8}$ oz. of shot, but from a knowledge of the total number of pellets per charge of shot (Table 4) and of the percentage in the 30-inch circle (Table 5) it is a simple matter to calculate the number of pellets in the 30-inch circle for loads or shot size other than those given in Table 5.

If you have worked out the probable number of pellets that will be on or close to the target under given conditions of choke, load and range you also need to know, if you wish the bird to be killed cleanly and not merely pricked, what will be the striking energy of those pellets. Small birds like snipe or woodcock can be killed by one or two pellets having a striking energy of only about $\frac{1}{2}$ ft lb.

A grouse would normally need three pellets with about $\frac{3}{4}$ ft lb. and a pheasant three with about 1 ft lb. striking energy, whereas for a large bird like a goose 4 pellets at $1\frac{1}{2}$ ft lb. is about the requirement. Table 7 (page 43) shows striking energies for various shot sizes.

Claims are sometimes made in articles and letters in sporting

7 Guns and cartridges 12-bore guns, and cartridges; with gun case, cartridge bag and cartridge belt

magazines of remarkably long shots. These are usually at wildfowl or pigeon since 'high' pheasants are often not as high as they seem; a pheasant 100 feet up is high enough for most of us and that is well within the 40-yards range. But you may read of a duck being killed at 60 yards, or a goose killed by a ·410 at 40 yards and of a pigeon dropped at '70 paces'. It cannot be over-emphasized that such shots should never have been attempted in the first place, still less should they be talked of afterwards. The cartridge manu-facturers are not entirely blameless, for they will quote 'effective ranges' for their cartridges which indicate that kills are possible at ranges of 45 or 50 yards. Such kills may be possible but they are not probable and these sort of statistics are apt to persuade young or inexperienced shots that their guns are more effective than any normal gun can be. 'Gun straining' is an all too common occur-rence on coastal marshes and foreshore, where reckless shooting at high birds results in many fowl being pricked, and also spoils the sport of other more patient gunners who are waiting hidden until such time as the duck or geese come in at a lower height.

It is a ballistic fact that shot pattern fails before striking energy. The fall in the number of pellets in the 30-inch circle at 50 yards compared with the number at 40 yards is about one-third, which is considerable. The normal 12-bore game gun should not, therefore, be used at a greater range than 40 yards; guns with $2\frac{3}{4}$- or 3-inch chambers, designed for wildfowling, can carry a bigger shot load and so produce a denser pattern at the longer ranges. The normal effective range of a ·410 with a $2\frac{1}{2}$-inch cartridge is about 30 yards and a 20 or 16-bore should be limited to about 35 yards.

A 30-inch circle, which is the conventional size when considering shot pattern, is not in fact very big for there is a great deal of sky all round it. Even a hare 26 inches long or a pheasant 30 inches long when placed precisely in the circle shows a good deal of space around it, and even more if only the vulnerable parts of the creature are considered. 100 pellets in such a circle may sound plenty but they can scatter themselves around so that most of them miss the target. See Figure 1(*a*). Any lesser number than 100 is far too thin a pattern, particularly when one remembers that the target will often, unfortunately, be partly outside the 30-inch circle where the pattern is much less dense. All of which emphasizes the need for accurate shooting. 160 pellets in the circle is more like the requirement and even that does not leave much margin for inaccuracy.

From the above information you ought to be able to decide what shot load and size of shot will suit your requirement, and the best thing to do is make your choice and stick to it. It is difficult to resist experimenting a little but if you dabble too much in shot sizes and carry a different size in each pocket the chances are that you will often be caught with the wrong one in the gun; it is sensible, however, to carry more than one size if, for instance, you are walking a marsh where snipe are to be expected (shot size no. 8) and you then intend to wait for duck flying in (shot size 5 or 4). But even the duck shooter can be worried: 'Teal might come in,' he thinks, 'They're pretty small, better have 7s for them. But a high old mallard will need a 4 to bring him down.'

So he puts no. 7 shot in his right barrel and no. 4 in his left. And in his pocket he has a few BB or no. 1s which he hurriedly pulls out and pops into the gun in place of the 7 and the 4 when

---

8. **The pattern plate**   The result on the pattern plate of two barrels. The centre of the pattern is at the top of the target, which is as it should be

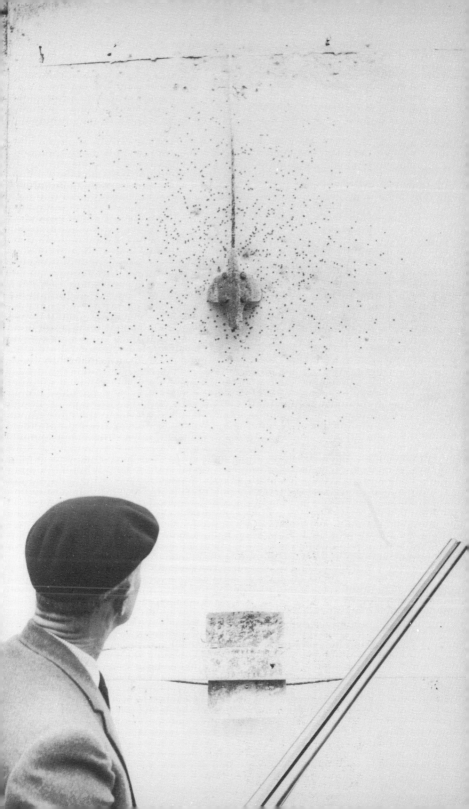

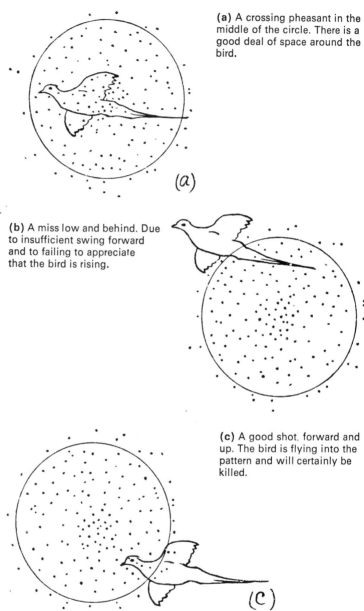

(a) A crossing pheasant in the middle of the circle. There is a good deal of space around the bird.

(b) A miss low and behind. Due to insufficient swing forward and to failing to appreciate that the bird is rising.

(c) A good shot, forward and up. The bird is flying into the pattern and will certainly be killed.

Figure 1   Pellets in the 30-inch circle

he hears the call of the geese! Shot fever is like that: there's usually some logic in the symptoms and its victims seem to enjoy their ailment, to the mystification of their untroubled shooting friends who usually ask for 6s when they buy cartridges, but are prepared to take more or less anything and shoot it off with careless abandon.

Shot loads and powders do, of course, influence the price of cartridges so that it is extravagant to use more of either than will do the job. But shot sizes cost the same in the same loading and it may be worth while for the enthusiast to check the patterning of his gun, for it is a fact that some guns, particularly old ones, do behave somewhat differently to their theoretical particulars given in the various Tables. Even new guns produce unusual patterns and cases have occurred where a gun which has the same boring for both barrels produces a correct pattern from one and a bad pattern from the other. Sometimes also a barrel will paradoxically produce a better pattern with, say, no. 5 shot than with no. 6. Therefore you should try your newly bought gun on the pattern plate, examine carefully the results and if they are not satisfactory return the gun to the makers for testing and correction.

A final word about range: few people can estimate range with much accuracy and unfortunately not many try to improve themselves in this respect. If you are going to teach yourself what a bird looks like at 25 yards and 40 yards you must know what that distance looks like on the ground; you should therefore know how your normal pace compares with a yard and this can be done over some known measured distance, such as on a small-bore rifle range or on a tennis court, which is 26 yards long. Perhaps you find that you take 30 paces to walk the length of a tennis court. Then, when you are pigeon shooting you can walk out 30 paces from your hide and note a tree or bush in the hedge which is about 25 yards from the hide. Similarly, 48 paces would indicate 40 yards. Until you are used to judging ranges it is a good plan to do this measuring quite frequently. At a pheasant stand, for instance, you could pace out the distance from your marker peg to the wood in front of you: suppose you find it is 30 yards and you estimate the height of the trees as 50 feet, then any bird flying just over the trees will be about 35 yards from you; if it is well above the trees it will be out of range until it comes over you. It is often edifying to select an object on the ground, such as a gate, a tussock of grass or a bush and decide how far away you reckon it is, and then pace the distance and see how far out you were. So you must learn to estimate ranges reasonably accurately, then to recognize various types of low-flying bird at different ranges and so to realize range *by what you can see of the bird*. At that stage you will be able to determine whether a bird in the sky, with no mark such as a tree near it, is in range or not, and you will be able to treat your cartridges fairly: shoot when the target is in range, leave it alone when it is not.

High-velocity cartridges were mentioned a few pages back. They are designed to provide greater hitting power at slightly longer ranges and particularly at tough targets like wildfowl. They are *not* meant to compensate a shooter for a slow swing by reaching the target quicker and so hitting a pheasant in the head instead of missing behind its tail. There actually are shooting men who, perhaps having fallen for some persuasive sales talk, really believe that high-velocity cartridges can magically turn misses into hits. Such is not the case; the calculated forward allowance to hit a bird crossing at 40 m.p.h. at 30 or 40 yards using high velocity cartridges is only 4 inches less than it is with standard velocity cartridges: 4 inches will not turn a miss into a hit.

Now for cartridge lengths, which may vary from 2 inches to 3 inches for 12-bore, and also for 16, 20, 28-bore and ·410; 8-bore cartridges may be $3\frac{1}{4}$ inches and 4-bore 4 inches. The important point here is the difference between the actual length of the completed cartridge and of its empty unloaded case, a difference which is amplified by the increasing popularity of the crimp closure for the front end of the cartridge. Crimp closure, by eliminating the front cardboard disc which held in the shot and the over-shot wad, is said to give more even and regular patterns, *but* crimp closure needs a greater length of case beyond the top of the shot charge to allow the end to be sealed than does the somewhat outdated rolled turnover. Therefore, if two empty cases are the same length and one is then crimped while the other is closed with a rolled turnover, the loaded crimped cartridge will be slightly the shorter. The fact to beware of is that the described length of a cartridge case is its length when empty, *not* its actual length when loaded, so that it is possible to load a cartridge described as '$2\frac{3}{4}$ inches' into a gun chambered, and therefore proofed, only for $2\frac{1}{2}$-inch cartridges.

In the days when all cartridges had a rolled turnover, it was generally reckoned that $1\frac{1}{8}$ or $1\frac{1}{16}$ oz. of shot went into a $2\frac{1}{2}$-inch case, 1¼oz, into a 2¾–inch case and 1⅜ or 1½ oz. into a 3-inch case. No one bothered to measure the length of a completed cartridge but had they done so they would have found that a '2½-inch' one measured about 2¼ inches and a '2¾-inch' slightly over 2½ inches. This did not much matter since the '2¾-inch' cartridge was known to contain more powder and shot than standard so that only a fool would try to put one into a 2½-inch chambered gun.

Most modern cartridges of British manufacture are described by the gauge size and by the length of gun chamber in which they are intended to be used, the description appearing on the cartridge box and sometimes also on the individual cartridge. The description does not refer to the actual length of the cartridge.

The length of a cartridge is not the same as the length of the chamber but, with rolled turn over cartridges, the length of the *fired case* is the same as the length of the chamber. With some crimp closure cartridges the length of the fired case is actually longer than the gun chamber; for instance, a number of 12 bore cartridges intended for 2½-inch chambers have cases which are 2¾ inches long. There are two reasons for this: with a case $2\frac{9}{16}$ inches long (12 bore, 2½-inch chambers are actually $2\frac{9}{16}$ inches long), the finished cartridge is only $2\frac{1}{16}$ inches long when crimp closed, as some of the tube is used for the closure. With such a short cartridge it is not always possible to accommodate the necessary length of wadding column for satisfactory ballistics, and so a longer case is necessary. The other reason concerns the correct functioning in auto-loading weapons. Many of these will feed only those loaded cartridges which are the same length as the old rolled turnover cartridges; a 2¾-inch case with a crimped closure gives this same length loaded as a $2\frac{9}{16}$-inch case with rolled turnover. There is no danger in using such cartridges with 2¾-inch cases in a 2½-inch chambered weapon because the loading of the cartridge is adjusted so that the ballistic level is satisfactory.

2½-inch cartridges are obviously made for 2½-inch chambered guns, but they can safely be used in 2¾-inch guns; they often are, when the owner of a 2¾-inch gun bought it because he wants the bigger shot load for wild-fowling but likes to use cheaper 2½-inch cartridges when he is, for instance, pigeon shooting. But cartridges *intended* for 2¾-inch chambers have higher pressures and they should not be used in 2½-inch guns. Similarly, cartridges intended for 3-inch chambers must not be used in shorter ones.

Progressive-burning powders permit heavier shot loads than

were common twenty years ago, and some American cartridges are loaded with $1\frac{5}{8}$ oz. in $2\frac{3}{4}$-inch cases and $1\frac{7}{8}$ oz. in 3-inch cases. These can generate alarmingly high pressures in guns not designed for them. In 1967 Imperial Metal Industries (Kynoch) Ltd, best known of British cartridge manufacturers, under the brand name of 'Eley', brought to the market their magnum cartridges. These have $1\frac{1}{2}$ oz. of shot in the $2\frac{3}{4}$-inch size and $1\frac{5}{8}$ oz. in the 3-inch size, and they created a certain stir, especially among the more sensible owners of 'Magnums', which in this case means not an extra large bottle of champagne but a 3-inch chambered gun used for wild-fowling. The new cartridges generated pressures higher than those for which most guns of similar chamber lengths were nitro-proved. The magnum cartridges can cause pressures up to $3\frac{1}{2}$ and 4 tons per square inch, respectively. Since 1955 the maximum service pressure for which a gun has been proved has been marked on the flats of the barrels (underneath, at the breech end!), but earlier guns are not so marked. If, therefore, you own a gun proved before 1955 you should check the service pressure which it can take before using 'magnum' cartridges. In fact, your old Magnum 3-inch gun, if in proof, will be safe with the $2\frac{3}{4}$-inch magnum cartridges, but it will require re-proof before using the 3-inch ones. When a gun is sent for a test proof the barrels must first be prepared by a gun-smith, who will ensure that they are really straight and will remove any dents; the gun will also be stripped and cleaned and the total cost is unlikely to be less than about £50. The owner of an oldish Magnum may well consider this price, and the possibility of his gun failing proof, not worth while, and so be content with restrict-ing himself to $2\frac{3}{4}$-inch magnum cartridges.

Between the powder charge and the shot load is the wadding, and all that need be said about it is that in the better modern cart-ridges this wadding is impregnated with a special cleansing com-pound so that the lead marks made in the bore by the shot are constantly wiped off. Similarly, good cartridges have a non-corros-ive cap or primer which results in there being no residue in the barrels which can cause rusting. Rust can still occur from rain and damp but these two advances in cartridge making greatly assist gun cleaning, and the days of boiling out barrels or using a wire mop known as a 'Turk's head' are virtually past. No sensible shooter would now accept cartridges which do not include these special wads and caps, just as he should also buy the best cart-ridges he can afford; cheap ones are nearly always a false economy.

Table 1 The main current Eley 12-bore game cartridges

Name	Shot charge, oz.	Suitable for guns with		Use
		Chamber length of:	and proved for pressures of	
Two inch	$\frac{7}{8}$	2 inches	$2\frac{3}{4}$ tons	Ultra light load
Impax	1	$2\frac{1}{2}$ inches	3 tons	Light load
Grand Prix	$1\frac{1}{16}$	$2\frac{1}{2}$ inches	3 tons	Normal game load
Grand Prix HV	$1\frac{1}{8}$	$2\frac{1}{2}$ inches	3 tons	Slightly bigger game load and high velocity
Maximum	$1\frac{3}{16}$	$2\frac{1}{2}$ inches	3 tons	Biggest load in $2\frac{1}{2}$-inch case, for wildfowling or high pheasants
Hymax	$1\frac{1}{4}$	$2\frac{3}{4}$ inches	$3\frac{1}{4}$ tons	Bigger load, without gun being too heavy
Alphamax	$1\frac{1}{4}$	$2\frac{3}{4}$ inches	$3\frac{1}{4}$ tons	As Hymax but slightly more expensive
Magnum 70	$1\frac{1}{2}$	$2\frac{3}{4}$ inches	$3\frac{1}{2}$ tons	Magnum, but $2\frac{3}{4}$-inch case
Magnum 75	$1\frac{5}{8}$	3 inches	4 tons	Heavier wildfowling gun, 3-inch case

Misfires rarely occur with modern cartridges but when one does it is most important that the shooter should look up the barrel before loading another cartridge. The misfire may be caused by a faulty firing pin, however it sometimes happens that the cap fires and the powder does not; it is even possible that the powder charge may be omitted through faulty loading. The small explosion of the cap could be sufficient to force the shot and wads into the barrel where they could lodge half-way up. If the misfired cartridge is then extracted and another one hurriedly loaded in order to shoot again as quickly as possible while the birds fly over, the result will be a burst barrel and probable injury to the shooter. Look through the barrels whenever there can be any doubt about them being clear, as for instance after struggling through a thick hedge or crawling through mud when wildfowling or standing around in the snow, but *always* have a look after a misfire.

Another possible cause of a misfire could be the inadvertent loading of a 20-bore cartridge into a 12-bore gun. The cartridge will slip through the chamber and lodge in the barrel and if a 12-bore cartridge is then loaded, the shooter having omitted to look up the barrel, a burst will surely follow. 20-bore cartridges can be a danger in this way and they should never be allowed to become mixed up with other sizes. Incidentally, to aid quick recognition of different bores, game cartridges normally come in various colours according to size, and in Great Britain these are crimson for heavy load 12 bore, orange for standard game load 12 bore, blue for 16 bore and yellow for 20 bore.

The method of carrying cartridges may be varied according to the shooter's requirements. For the rough shooter a cartridge belt is convenient and the best type has leather sockets the full length of the cartridge, which will then be protected from damp. Belts with a narrow webbing strap about ¾ inch wide, or with metal clips for the cartridges are not so satisfactory. The belt wearer should in any case put his belt under his coat in rain. A cartridge bag is convenient for carrying ammunition on an organized shoot at driven birds, and most shooters find it convenient to put the bag on the ground at each stand and to have a dozen or so cartridges in the jacket side-pocket for easy loading. A leather bag is expensive, but much better than a canvas one; leather lasts a lifetime or more and will keep out the wet. When a loader is used he will carry the cartridge bag and he may have some sort of gadget for carrying a few rounds ready for quick loading. (This is discussed on pages 141–6.) Those not used to carrying many cartridges around may care to know that 100 12-bore game cartridges weigh 10 lb.

Explosives should always be treated with respect but there is not much to be afraid of about shotgun cartridges outside a gun. As an explosive they are listed as 'not liable to explode in bulk' although that is not sufficient for the Post Office to allow them to be sent through the post. Nevertheless, there is no danger of cartridges in one's pocket exploding due to being jolted together. If by some freak chance a cartridge cap was fired in the pocket the powder would burn, not explode, and the shot and wads would not be discharged in a harmful way but would either remain in the case or simply fall out of the end. Pipe smokers who are apt in

a forgetful moment to stuff a still-smouldering pipe into their cartridge pockets may take solace from this information; they might
well suffer a burnt jacket but they do not run the risk of receiving
a charge of shot in the hip. You may like to experiment and see
the effect of a cartridge discharged outside a gun: place one on the
ground, base towards you, and shoot at it from about 10 yards.
When the cap is struck the powder will burn but the shot will not
be discharged. Try it and see! You will then have convinced yourself that an explosion needs confinement, as of course is the case
with petrol in a motor car engine. Petrol and powder, when not
confined, merely burn.

Storing cartridges should raise no problem provided common
sense is used. In their manufacture they are subjected to tests by
storing them in temperatures varying from —5° to +55° C. A
cupboard where the temperature is reasonably even provides perfectly adequate storing in any normal house, and cartridges can
be kept thus for years. If cartridges have become wet they should
be dried out slowly in gentle warmth and not subjected to such
intense heat as being put in the oven or on the kitchen stove.
Slow drying will allow the swollen cases to contract to their original
size and no harm will be done.

As with most things, nowadays, there are gimmicks in cartridge
making too. Fall for them if you will, they are fairly harmless, but
do not pay extra money for them. Half sizes in shot is an example:
one ounce of no. 6 shot contains 270 pellets, one ounce of no. 7
has 340 pellets and $6\frac{1}{2}$ shot gives us 300. If you think you can have
the best of both worlds by using $6\frac{1}{2}$ shot then by all means use it,
but do not imagine it is going to have any noticeable effect on
your shooting. Neither will 'Special Straight Shot' loading or any
other miraculous concoction worked out by some small-town
cartridge seller who buys his cases with his name printed on them
and then tries to load them better than the big, highly efficient
factories. Some years ago one of these 'little men' did manage to
do good business, through the clever use of a gimmick. This, in
the days of the rolled turnover, was simply to use a transparent
top to the cartridge instead of the normal cardboard disc. 'Look,'
said his customers to one another, 'You can see the shot! Must be
good!' And they ordered many more of the same brand.

Do not blame your cartridges if you miss, but do understand
enough about them to ensure that you use the type most suitable
for your sort of shooting.

Table 2   Standard shot loads for smokeless powders, as used in standard factory-loaded cartridges

Bore	Gun chamber length (inches)	Shot charge (ounces)	Bore	Gun chamber length (inches)	Shot charge (ounces)
4	4	3	12	2	$\frac{7}{8}$
8	$3\frac{1}{4}$	2	16	$2\frac{3}{4}$	$1\frac{1}{8}$
10	$2\frac{7}{8}$	$1\frac{7}{16}$	16	$2\frac{1}{2}$	$\frac{15}{16}$
10	$2\frac{5}{8}$	$1\frac{5}{16}$	20	$2\frac{3}{4}$	1
12	3	$1\frac{3}{8}$	20	$2\frac{1}{2}$	$\frac{13}{16}$
12	$2\frac{3}{4}$	$1\frac{1}{4}$	28	$2\frac{1}{2}$	$\frac{9}{16}$
12	$2\frac{1}{2}$	$1\frac{3}{16}$	·410	3	$\frac{11}{16}$
12	$2\frac{1}{2}$	$1\frac{1}{8}$	·410	$2\frac{1}{2}$	$\frac{7}{16}$
12	$2\frac{1}{2}$	$1\frac{1}{16}$	·410	2	$\frac{5}{16}$
12	$2\frac{1}{2}$	1			

Table 3   Approximate comparison of shot sizes

Metric (mm)	English	American and Swedish	French	Belgian and Dutch	Italian	Spanish
9·1	LG	–	–	–	–	–
8·4	SG	OO Buck	–	9G	11/0	–
7·6	Special SG	1 Buck	C2	12G	9/0	–
6·8	SSG	3 Buck	C3	–	–	–
5·2	AAA	4 Buck	5/0	–	–	–
4·1	BB	air rifle	1	OO	OO	1
3·6	1	2	3	–	1 or 2	3
3·3	3	4	4	–	3	4
3·1	4	5	5	–	4	5
2·8	5	6	6	5	5	6
2·6	6	–	–	6	6	–
2·4	7	$7\frac{1}{2}$	7	7	7	7
2·3	$7\frac{1}{2}$	8	$7\frac{1}{2}$	$7\frac{1}{2}$	$7\frac{1}{2}$	$7\frac{1}{2}$
2·2	8	–	8	8	8	8
2·0	9	9	9	9	9	9

Table 4   Pellets in game charges

Ounces of shot	Size of shot					
	3	4	5	6	7	8
$1\frac{1}{2}$	210	255	330	405	510	675
$1\frac{7}{16}$	201	244	316	388	489	646
$1\frac{3}{8}$	192	234	303	371	468	618
$1\frac{5}{16}$	183	223	289	354	446	590
$1\frac{1}{4}$	175	213	275	338	425	562
$1\frac{3}{16}$	166	202	261	321	404	534
$1\frac{1}{8}$	157	191	248	304	383	506
$1\frac{1}{16}$	149	181	234	287	361	478
ONE	140	170	220	270	340	450
$\frac{15}{16}$	131	159	206	253	319	422
$\frac{7}{8}$	122	149	193	236	298	394
$\frac{13}{16}$	113	138	179	219	276	366
$\frac{3}{4}$	105	128	165	202	255	338
$\frac{11}{16}$	96	117	151	186	234	310
$\frac{5}{8}$	87	106	138	169	212	282
$\frac{9}{16}$	78	96	124	152	191	254
$\frac{1}{2}$	70	85	110	135	170	225

Table 5   Percentage of total pellets in 30-inch circle

Boring of gun	Range (yards)				
	30	35	40	45	50
True cylinder	60	49	40	33	27
Improved cylinder	72	60	50	41	33
$\frac{1}{4}$ choke	77	65	55	46	38
$\frac{1}{2}$ choke	83	71	60	50	41
$\frac{3}{4}$ choke	91	77	65	55	46
Full choke	100	84	70	59	49

Table 6 Number of pellets in 30-inch circle, standard loads

$(1\frac{1}{16}$ SHOT) $(1\frac{1}{8}$ SHOT)

Gun boring	Range (yards)					Gun boring	Range (yards)				
	30	35	40	45	50		30	35	40	45	50
No. 4 shot						No. 4 shot					
(181 pellets)						(191 pellets)					
True cylinder	109	89	72	60	49	True cylinder	115	94	76	63	52
Improved cyl.	130	109	91	74	60	Improved cyl.	138	115	96	78	63
¼ choke	139	118	100	83	69	¼ choke	147	124	105	88	73
½ choke	150	129	109	91	74	½ choke	159	136	115	96	78
¾ choke	165	139	118	100	83	¾ choke	174	147	124	105	88
Full choke	181	152	127	107	89	Full choke	191	160	134	113	94
No. 5 shot						No. 5 shot					
(234 pellets)						(248 pellets)					
True cylinder	140	115	94	77	63	True cylinder	149	122	99	82	67
Improved cyl.	168	140	117	96	77	Improved cyl.	179	149	124	102	82
¼ choke	180	152	129	108	89	¼ choke	191	161	136	114	94
½ choke	194	166	140	117	96	½ choke	206	176	149	124	102
¾ choke	213	180	152	129	108	¾ choke	226	191	161	136	114
Full choke	234	196	164	138	115	Full choke	248	208	174	146	122
No. 6 shot						No. 6 shot					
(287 pellets)						(304 pellets)					
True cylinder	172	141	115	95	77	True Cylinder	182	149	122	100	82
Improved cyl.	207	172	144	118	95	Improved cyl.	219	182	152	125	100
¼ choke	221	187	158	132	109	¼ choke	234	198	167	140	116
½ choke	238	204	172	144	118	½ choke	252	216	182	152	125
¾ choke	261	221	187	158	132	¾ choke	277	234	198	167	140
Full choke	287	241	201	169	141	Full choke	304	255	213	179	149
No. 7 shot						No. 7 shot					
(361 pellets)						(383 pellets)					
True cylinder	217	177	144	119	97	True cylinder	230	188	153	126	103
Improved cyl.	260	217	181	148	119	Improved cyl.	276	230	191	157	126
¼ choke	278	235	199	166	137	¼ choke	295	249	211	176	146
½ choke	299	256	217	181	148	½ choke	318	272	230	191	157
¾ choke	329	278	235	199	166	¾ choke	349	295	249	211	176
Full choke	361	303	253	213	177	Full choke	383	322	268	226	188

The number of pellets for other loads and shot sizes may be calculated, using tables 4 and 5

e.g.

With a load of 1¼ oz. and No. 3 shot, what is pattern at 50 yards with full choke?

Answer: From Table 4, number of pellets = 175

From Table 5, full choke at 50 yards gives 49% within 30-inch circle

Therefore pattern is $\dfrac{49 \times 175}{100}$

= 85·75, say 86, pellets.

Table 7 Striking energy in foot-pounds for individual pellets. Standard Game Cartridges

Size of shot	*Range (yards)*					
	20	30	35	40	45	50
3	5·79	4·48	3·92	3·43	2·99	2·59
4	4·68	3·54	3·08	2·66	2·30	1·97
5	3·52	2·60	2·23	1·90	1·61	1·36
6	2·80	2·03	1·71	1·44	1·20	1·01
7	2·16	1·52	1·27	1·06	0·86	0·70

Number 6 shot has a striking energy of about 1 ft lb. at 50 yards; therefore it would be able to kill a pheasant at that range. But pattern fails before striking energy and kills at more than 40 yards are flukes rather than clever shooting.

3 Gun fitting

Your gun must fit you. If it does not, your ability to shoot straight with it is immediately handicapped.

A first class shot can hit the target with practically any gun, but he knows enough about guns and shooting to see at once the shape of the gun in his hands and to mount it accordingly. But the ordinary shot needs to concentrate only on the bird he is shooting at and to know that his gun will follow his eye and shoot precisely where he is pointing it; his ability to point it in the right direction is another matter and instruction on this follows in later chapters.

If you already own a gun you can make some simple tests of its fit by fixing up an aiming mark, such as a piece of paper pinned to a tree, and then putting up the gun at it quickly with both eyes open. When the gun is up, close your left eye and check where it is pointing: if it is high there is probably not enough bend in the stock, and if low then the stock is bent too much; if the gun points left you need more cast-off and if to the right the amount of cast-off should be reduced. See Photographs 1 and 2 for illustrations of what is meant by 'bend' and 'cast-off'. If the stock tends to catch in your clothing as you bring it up it is too long. A short stock causes an unnatural position for the left arm, but its effect will be especially noticeable when the gun is fired because then the butt will not be bedded properly into the shoulder and the recoil will cause discomfort and bruising. You can also check the alignment of your eye along the gun by pointing the gun at your own eye in a mirror; if the gun is properly mounted and fitting correctly your right eye should be exactly along the rib with the whole of the eye visible above the breech (Photograph 6).

If you are in any doubt about the fit of your gun you should take it to a qualified gun fitter, usually to be found in a Shooting School. You should do the same when you buy a gun, new or second-hand and you *must* go for a fitting to ascertain your measurements, if you are having a gun made for you.

44

Fitting is done by using a pattern-plate and a try-gun. The plate is usually steel at least 6 ft high and 12 ft wide and it is covered with whitewash except for a central black mark. The impressions made by shotgun pellets can easily be seen on the whitewash so that the general pattern may be judged, and also the individual pellets can be counted when the performance of a gun's barrels is being tested, which is normally done at 40 yards range (Photograph 8). The try-gun has an adjustable stock, and screws behind the breech can be altered to move the stock more or less to the right, when viewed from above; this is cast-off, which is necessary to compensate for the fact that the right shoulder is a few inches further to the right than is the right eye, and were the stock truly straight the gun would lie slightly across the body and so shoot to the left. For shooting from the left shoulder cast-on would be required and this can also be arranged on the try-gun. Further screws by the hand grip allow the stock to be raised or lowered and so alter the amount of bend. Normal measurements for bend (also sometimes called 'drop') are $1\frac{1}{2}$ inches at the comb and 2 inches at the heel of the stock, the heel sometimes being called the 'bump'. Normal cast-off is $\frac{1}{8}$ inch at the comb, and $\frac{1}{4}$ inch at the bump and toe. The comb of the try-gun can be raised or lowered and the butt can be extended to alter the whole length of the stock.

The method of fitting consists of setting the try-gun to standard measurements and then letting the customer fire a few shots at the pattern-plate at about 25 yards. By altering cast-off and bend, the fitter makes the gun shoot where the gunner is pointing and, indeed, where he is *looking*, for in shotgun shooting you do not aim the gun: you look at a target and then point at it. The fitter's job is to see that if you do this, with both eyes open, when you throw up your left hand with a gun in it the muzzles will be pointing precisely where you are looking. The correct stock length is best found by the person being fitted firing several shots at a simple clay-pigeon going straight away from him. You concentrate on shooting and the fitter watches to see how the butt comes up into your shoulder. He can see if the heel sticks up too high, by observing from behind, or if the toe is too low below the shoulder. He will also be watching to see how the actual shape of the butt beds into your shoulder. The shape is determined by what is called 'stand', and this is measured on a gun by placing it on the floor with toe and heel of the butt in contact with the ground and the breech just touching a vertical post; the distance the top of the rib at the muzzle is away from the post is the 'stand' for the gun. If the toe of the butt is very prominent the stand may be such that the muzzles are over perpendicular and this is sometimes necessary in order to make some shooters keep their gun muzzles high enough to be on a target straight out in front of them; the prominent toe would not be a handicap in overhead shots because then it is scarcely in contact with the shoulder.

If you buy a second-hand gun the dealer may suggest, while you are examining several weapons, that a way to check the correct length of stock is to grip the gun in the small of the butt with the right hand, place the index finger over the right trigger and see if the butt fits into the lower part of your biceps when your arm is bent at a right angle. This is only a very rough guide and is not at all reliable; it also takes no account of the shape of the butt. Only proper gun fitting can give you the stock you require.

The fitter will also require to see you shooting at an oncoming clay-pigeon, taking it straight overhead. If the try-gun stock is too long it will show up at once on this shot because you will find it difficult to reach up comfortably, and either the butt will come into your shoulder too low down or your left hand will slide back along the barrels. Adjustments can be made again until the stock comes neatly into your shoulder and those high shots can be taken with no strain.

A final check will be made that the gun barrels align correctly with your aiming eye and for this you will point the gun, having checked that it is unloaded, at the gun fitter's eye. He can then see that there is a straight line from his eye, all the way down the rib of the gun to your eye and that the stock fits naturally into your shoulder.

The settings on the try-gun can now be measured and applied to the new gun you are ordering or they may be put on your present ill-fitting gun by a qualified gunsmith.

The main measurements are:

Cast-off;
Bend;
Length of stock (to bump, centre and toe, to account for stand).

Now, there are further small fitting features which can influence the comfort and speed with which you can mount and fire your gun. First, the comb: this should be the right height so that the top of the stock comes comfortably to the cheek when the gun is in

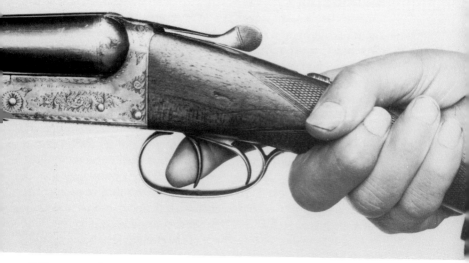

9 **Finger on the trigger: right** The pad of the forefinger on the trigger, thumb well round the grip

10 **Finger on the trigger: wrong** Finger hooked too far round the second trigger, second finger touching the trigger guard, thumb on top of the stock and in danger of being jabbed by the top lever, especially as the base of the thumb is not bedded against the comb

the firing position, and there must be no need for the shooter to drop his head down sideways a little in order to reach the top of the stock. The comb on the try-gun is therefore adjustable and it sometimes needs raising above the standard height for fitting someone whose neck is longer than average; this does not affect the measurement at the bump. The actual position of the end of the comb is important because if it is too far forward it will obtrude on to the base of the thumb when the gun is gripped at the small of the butt; should it do so a small piece can be taken off and this is the sort of simple fitting that can improve the comfort of a ready-made or second-hand gun which has not been fitted to the user.

When the right hand is gripping the gun the safety catch should be situated so that it is convenient for the thumb to slide it forward, but not situated so far back that, after it has been pushed off, the catch comes underneath the base of the thumb. When this occurs there is a likelihood that the recoil on firing one barrel may cause the base of the thumb to jerk the safety catch on again and so prevent the second barrel from being fired. The precise location of the safety catch between the back of the top lever and the front of the comb varies with different guns and it is a point to look out for when buying a second-hand gun; the position cannot be altered once the catch has been fixed in the stock but if you are buying a ready-made gun you will do well to check that the position is satisfactory, and if your gun is being made for you, see that the catch is far enough forward on the grip to be comfortable.

With the right hand firmly on the grip of the gun your index finger should be able to reach the right trigger, using the pad above the first finger joint and not hooking the trigger into the bend of the joint. In this position the rear of the trigger guard must be clear of your second finger so that this finger does not become bruised on recoil. Here is another feature to look for when buying a ready-made gun (Photographs 9 and 10).

The actual thickness and shape of the grip is important because only if it fills the hand can the latter hold it firmly. Too thin a grip will allow the gun to slip back on recoil and can cause a bruised second finger, even though the finger was initially clear of the trigger guard. The length and thickness of the grip must suit the size of the hand which is to hold it. Occasionally the index finger is bruised by the front trigger when it is on the back trigger, and if this is persistent it may be overcome by fitting a hinged front trigger which can bend forward and so not hit against the finger. Similarly, a rubber ring can be put on the back of the trigger guard to protect the second finger, but correct gun fitting is better than these last-resort remedies.

It has been said that a gun must fit its owner as well as his clothes, and this implies that his clothes must fit him too. If you are going to shoot well you must see that all your equipment is arranged so that none of it handicaps you in the already difficult enough task of shooting straight. You have the best gun you can afford and good cartridges and your clothes should likewise be designed for the job.

Wear a hat, with an all-round brim to protect your eyes and to prevent rain from running down the back of your neck. Have a good tweed jacket cut generously at the back of the shoulders, and not a somewhat tight-waisted sports coat. Shooting jackets sometimes have pleats behind the shoulders or down the middle of the back and some tailors have their own special methods of cutting, which allow free movement of the shoulders; plenty of room at the elbows and pivot sleeves are often incorporated. The essential features of your jacket are that it shall be easy and offer no restriction when you raise your arms above your head, and that its material shall be thick enough to keep out the rain. You may wear a mackintosh between drives and perhaps when walking-up, but to show your best performance at the covert side you need to be prepared to shed the top coat and shoot in your proper jacket: the jacket you wore when you were fitted for your gun, or at least a copy of it. You will, of course, bring your shooting jacket to the Shooting School when you attend for gun fitting, and not expect to be fitted wearing a lounge suit, or indeed anything else but what you intend to shoot in.

We are considering now only that aspect of clothing which affects your ability to shoot so we need not discuss the colour of your tweeds or your waistcoat, but it is worth stating that your clothes should keep you warm even when standing about in a biting east wind. So keep your hands warm. You can use mittens, of which there are several patterns on the market, designed for shooting; or you can use ordinary leather gloves with the top of the right index finger half cut through at the first joint. This allows the top inch or so of the glove to be folded back off the finger where it can be retained by a press stud, the two halves being sewn on to the top of the end of the glove finger and on to the top of its middle joint respectively. The end of your finger is then bare to feel for the trigger, and you can undo the stud and push the glove back on again to keep the finger warm between drives when you are not shooting.

Boots ought to be large enough to allow thick socks to be worn and they must have studs in the soles so that you do not slip on wet ground. Many people nowadays wear gumboots for shooting, perhaps because they are comfortable and easy to clean. But rubber boots can be uncomfortable if you have to do much walking and they are cold for standing around in the snow. It is worth noting that composition-soled gumboots with studs can now be obtained; they are cut narrower in the leg and instep than ordinary gumboots and for all types of shooting except wildfowling they are excellent. Clothing for wildfowlers is a special subject and one on which 'fowlers themselves will argue interminably. There is a chapter on it in *The New Wildfowler in the 70s* (Barrie & Jenkins, 1979).

4 Gun mounting

We have stressed the importance of gun fitting but even more important is the complex business of gun mounting, which requires a correct stance, and grip, and aim and a stylish technique to co-ordinate all the movements. If you can master the several actions in correct gun mounting you will be able to shoot reasonably well with any gun under any circumstances. For top performance, and especially for quick shooting at driven game, correct fitting is essential but a made-to-measure gun is of no help if the man who uses it has not learnt how to handle it.

The stance should be comfortable and it may vary according to the build of the shooter, but the feet need to be fairly close together and the general attitude must be that of a half-turn to the right front. (Common faults are feet too far apart and the right foot forward, nearly alongside the left so that the shooter's chest is almost facing his target instead of being at an angle of about 45° to the line of fire.) Nearly all the weight is on the left foot, the right heel is just clear of the ground and a slight forward lean induces a feeling of mild resistance in the left hip; it is not a tension, for the whole body from the hips up must be able to rotate right or left for slightly more than a right angle without the feet being moved. The left knee is not bent and it is the only joint that is kept stiff during the rotating movements. This swinging from side to side is worth practising with the arms held out horizontally in front of you, keeping the left hand nearly opposite the right; this is more difficult when pivoting to the left, but that does not matter since, when shooting, the left arm is in front of the right as your chest remains obliquely to your front; then you can do it holding the gun and this ought to impress on you how you *can* get your *body* round to face the target and that it is wrong to wave your arm across your body and turn your head; see Figure 2 for correct stance.

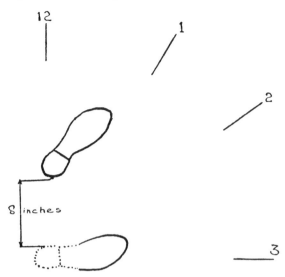

Figure 2   The correct position for the feet, the shooter's front being towards twelve o'clock

Balance should remain perfect throughout these rotational movements and the gun barrels must stay level. It is not correct to shift the weight to the right foot and to raise the left heel when swinging to the right because this can so easily result in the gun being canted over sideways, especially on a high shot.

Correct stance is more easily found on a firm lawn in the garden than on the varied ground experienced in a day's shooting but it is important always to try to have your feet planted firmly and evenly on the ground. When waiting for driven game you should stamp out as level a platform as you can, particularly if you are standing on a slope or on uneven ground such as plough. Footwork is often a neglected part of shooting technique and if you study action photographs you will notice how many people move their feet incorrectly. The question of when and how the feet ought to be moved will be dealt with when describing the various types of shot in later chapters.

---

11 Shooting in gloves   A good reach up for a bird approaching fairly high. Left hand in front of the fore-end. The shooter is wearing gloves, with the trigger finger bared. His left knee ought to be a little stiffer. Useful looking labrador

The gun should be gripped firmly with the right hand at the small of the butt, sometimes called the 'grip' or the 'hand'. It is a good, solid hold which could raise the gun to the shoulder without using the left hand at all. The left hand has an entirely different sort of grip which varies from a loose hold through which the gun can slide to a firm nip between fingers and thumb, but not using the palm of the hand to grasp the gun.

Before arranging the position of the left hand on the gun let us consider the vital function of that hand in aiming the gun. Please try a little experiment: stick your left hand out in front of you and point at any object with the forefinger. There is an automatic co-ordination between eye and finger and both are concentrated on the same object. Now turn over the palm of your left hand and extend the thumb straight out and slightly to the left. Your left hand and arm are now pretty well in the correct position for holding and pointing your gun.

The left hand is always thrust out at your target. Its hold initially, from wherever it was on the gun while you were at rest, is light and the barrels can slide through it; this hand moves first in mounting the gun and it puts the muzzles on the target and holds them there while the butt remains down. Then, as the right hand brings up the stock to the shoulder and cheek the barrels slide through the fingers of the left hand, which grips them when the butt is in the shoulder; the attitude of the left hand is with the thumb lying along the left barrel, the first finger running up between and underneath the two barrels – pointing – and the three remaining fingers gripping the right barrel along its side. There should be no finger or thumb over the top of either barrel and no weight in the palm of the hand.

If a finger or thumb of the left hand does intrude on to the top of the gun barrels the effect on shooting can be remarkable, so much so that if you visit a shooting school it is worth while trying to see the unfortunate result. If the thumb comes over the left barrel your line of sight, instead of running straight up the centre of the barrels over the rib, will be deflected up the right barrel, which means that the barrels are sighted slightly to the right and you will miss to that side; should the fingers appear over the right barrel the converse applies and the shot misses to the left.

Some shooting men adopt what may be called the 'heavy' grip with the left hand, when they have the weight of the gun heavily in the left palm, and fingers and thumb over the top edges of the barrels. They can still see along the rib and they may be able to shoot straight, but this grip is not recommended because it makes the hold on the barrels feel heavy and sluggish whereas what we want is a light and lively grip which will allow us to push the gun around the sky and point it quickly at our target. The best left hand grip is indeed really a 'nip' between thumb and three fingers, with the index finger touching the barrels, not bearing weight, and pointing at the target.

Beginners nearly always hold a gun with the left hand too far back, and if they also adopt a heavy grip and have fingers and thumb on top of the barrels, they tend to try to look over the top so that sighting becomes wildly erratic (Photograph 74). There is no specific position along the barrels where the left hand must be positioned but a straight or very nearly straight arm is recommended since it gives better balance for the gun, keeps the muzzles up and is the natural position for pointing. The closer grip with a bent left elbow is usually adopted because the shooter has graduated to the shotgun from the rifle and he thinks in terms of a tight hold and aiming, instead of a freely moving left arm and pointing. It is worth remembering that on a standard game gun the fore-end was put there to hold the gun together, *not* to accommodate the owner's left hand. His hand might comfortably fit over the fore-end but it is more likely that his forefinger will be in front of it, on the metal of the barrels.

Now, with your stance correct, a knowledge of how to grip the gun and of what we mean by aiming, you will need to practise mounting the gun, which calls for co-ordination of eye and brain with movements of arms and body, and perhaps feet as well. Mounting starts when the target is first seen: the correct stance is taken, with the left foot pointing at about 1 o'clock from the target; the left hand pushes out the barrels towards the bird so that you can watch it past the muzzles, and as the bird swings to either side of you so does your body pivot and allow the muzzles to stay on; at this stage the stock is lying along the lower forearm, with the butt by your elbow; as the right hand then brings up the butt the left arm thrusts out, gripping the barrels, and for a fraction of a second the gun is at eye level and the butt is just touching the shoulder but not bedded firmly against it, and at this critical moment your shoulder comes forward to meet the butt; as the butt comes hard into the shoulder you squeeze the trigger. During the whole movement your body is pivoting as required by the movement of the bird and your gun muzzles are swinging with it and being raised by the left hand to keep them on target.

The mounting of the gun is a deliberate, smooth and comparatively slow movement and the body is relaxed until the instant of firing. As the gun meets the shoulder the left arm is pulling it forward and this, combined with the tight grip of the right hand and the thrust forward of the shoulder, results in practically no recoil being felt. The cheek must be bedded closely on the stock and the head held normally erect, not bent down to get the eye low nor bent back in instinctive fear of the shock of discharge. As the gun is fired the left knee is stiff and the shoulder and neck muscles are tensed but the hips remain fluid and continue the swing of body and gun barrels. Both elbows should be in a natural midway position, not pointing down to the ground and not stuck out horizontally. Common mistakes with beginners are to relax their grip at the moment of firing, to draw away their heads or shoulders and to flinch, all of which, besides ensuring a miss, also result in the recoil giving them a blow on the shoulder or even on the upper biceps when the butt has slipped; sometimes a smack in the mouth from the top of the stock can also be caused in this way. Have no fear when you fire a gun; hold it firmly, be determined to master it and have confidence that you are going to point it in the right direction and pull the trigger exactly when you want to.

One talks of mounting a gun slowly but it is really the deliberateness that needs emphasizing. If you watch a good shot in action he appears to be slow because he is precise and his movements are not hasty and jerked. Your mounting must also be slow but it must finish with a snap; you are leaning forward a bit as you mount the gun, you keep your eye unwaveringly on the target but when your gun *is* up you fire at once, with no dawdling about waving your gun across the sky in pursuit of your bird. If you see a shooter hanging in the aim like that with his gun muzzles following a bird you can be practically certain he is going to miss. It is very bad style and even if its followers sometimes score a hit they really scarcely deserve to.

Basically, then, gun mounting consists of (Photographs 12–17):

1   Eye picks up bird and body pivots with it.
2   Left hand puts muzzle on, butt still down.
3   Right hand brings up butt slowly, while body and left hand keep muzzle on line of flight.

4 Shoulder comes into butt and gun is fired.

Under the general heading of gun mounting we may examine several smaller movements which occur in handling and which can affect safety and efficiency.

When should you put the safety catch to the firing position? Basically, the answer is 'only just before the trigger is pulled'. You should certainly *not* have the safety catch off while you are sitting or standing waiting for birds to appear. The correct time to push forward the safety slide is as you prepare for your shot and this means that three things happen simultaneously:

1 Weight on the left foot in the direction of the bird.
2 Muzzle in line with the bird; stock still down along the forearm;
3 Safety slide pushed forward.

You then carry on mounting the gun and take the shot *but*, if the bird does not after all come into range, or if someone else shoots it, your immediate reaction as you lower the gun must be to push the slide back to 'safe'. While you are in the ready position, and you are pushing the safety catch off, it is most important that your right forefinger should be along the trigger guard and it must not move on to the trigger until the next stage when you bring the butt to your shoulder. If you allow your finger to stray on to the trigger too soon there is every possibility that the action of pushing off the safety catch with your thumb will result in a corresponding movement back of your finger, and the gun will go off. Besides being potentially dangerous to others this can result in the top lever jabbing back on recoil and cutting the top of your thumb. To avoid risk of this injury the thumb should be trained to flick back to the side of the grip immediately it has operated the safety catch.

It is sometimes advocated that the safety catch should be pushed off as the gun is mounted, but this can be dangerous because the thumb may again be caught by the top lever if the gun is fired a little too quickly; it can also be frustrating if the thumb is a bit slow and the finger tries to pull the trigger before the thumb has managed to work the catch. So play safe and set the safety catch for firing as you prepare for a shot, and remember to keep your trigger finger along the guard.

Another important little movement in gun handling is that of the finger on the trigger. The pull should be practically unnoticed,

Preparing for the shot

12 *Top left* If, when taking a horizontal shot, you throw up the gun directly from this waiting position –

13 *Top right* – the chances are that the muzzle will initially be a bit too high –

16 *Bottom* – and keep the muzzle on the line eye to target, as the butt comes up

14 *Top left* – or too low. The result is that the muzzle waves up and down, seeking the target, and this must be unsettling to the shot

15 *Top Right* From the waiting position you should prepare for the shot like this: gun partially raised, muzzle on the bird –

17 *Bottom* Then your muzzle will be right on target as your shoulder comes to the butt, and you can fire immediately, on first aim. Note that most shooters would do better to have their left arms straighter which means that when the brain says, 'Fire!' the forefinger contracts on the trigger and the shooter is immediately aware that the gun has gone off. This may all sound obvious but the point is that for such a satisfactory state of affairs to occur the weight of the trigger pulls must be correct. The subject was mentioned briefly on page 16 when standard trigger pulls were given as about $3\frac{1}{2}$ and 4 lb., the left barrel always being a bit heavier than the right because its trigger position allows the finger to obtain greater leverage so that it feels correspondingly lighter, and also because the movement on to the second trigger is usually harsher and quicker than on to the first. Trigger pulls can work out of adjustment and they can be wrong in newly acquired second-hand guns, and so you can appreciate that this is a point to watch, or at least to be aware of, because although trigger troubles are not very common they can be increasingly important as the skill of the shooter increases. Too light a trigger pull can result in shots going off too soon, before the shooter is properly on his target, and they are also a source of danger; too heavy a pull may cause the gun to be dragged off its target as the shooter struggles to haul back the trigger.

The weight of a trigger pull should be heavier with a heavy gun than with a light one, although the feel to the user will be the same. Some very good shots with sensitive hands like to have light trigger pulls and they need the best locks for this; only a good side-lock can provide an unvarying and sharp pull as light as about 2 lb. The more skilful shot does develop an increasing awareness of trigger pulls, particularly if he uses more than one gun. When a pair of guns is used, it is essential that the pulls on each pair shall be the same, otherwise the user will notice the difference at once. The average shooting man need not worry much about trigger pulls; they do affect gun handling, but only when the shooter is aware that something feels odd is there any necessity to take action and check the pulls.

The balance of any piece of sporting equipment that is held in the hand affects the man who uses it, and fishermen and tennis players, cricketers and golfers all pay attention to the balance of their rods and racquets, bats and clubs. So also is the balance of a gun of interest to a shooter. But do not think 'balance' literally refers to a place on a gun where it can be balanced, see-sawing gently up and down if supported only at that spot. You may meet gun-knowledgeable characters who take your gun, place a finger under the joint pin joining the barrels to the stock and allow the gun to balance there for a moment, unsupported through the rest of its length. According to whether the muzzle or the butt dips down they mutter sagely: 'Well balanced gun, that one,' or, 'Don't like it, seems heavy in the stock,' but these remarks are nonsense. Your gun is correctly balanced for you if it feels right when you mount it.

It is difficult for the novice to know what a right 'feel' of a gun is like, just as the newcomer to tennis has little idea of how the balance of his racquet ought to feel. But a little experience soon gives him the idea. The balance of a gun varies with different people and you can tell whether it is nicely balanced for you by picking it up, holding it loosely in both hands for a moment, and then mounting it. If the muzzle seems to 'ask' to go forward and up, then that gun suits you, but if it feels heavy and clumsy in front and does not 'want' to go where you wish to put it the balance is wrong, for you, but it is not necessarily a badly balanced gun. Your gun must feel right in your hands and if the balance seems easy and pleasant, mounting will be helped and shooting will benefit.

Eyesight controls shotgun shooting in as much as that the whole object of correct gun mounting is to make the gun point where the eye is looking. With most people the right eye is master, but sometimes both eyes take equal control and sometimes the left is the stronger. You can do a simple test to see whether your right eye is the master by extending your right arm to the front and pointing at an object with your forefinger, both eyes being open; now close your left eye and look along your arm and finger as if it was a rifle and you will probably find the finger is still pointing at the object because, although you had both eyes open, the right took control. If, however, your left is master eye you will find, when you close it, that your finger seems to be pointing well to the left of your target; now close the right eye and open the left and the finger is pointing true, as you thought you had aimed originally, showing that your left eye took control (Photograph 18).

It is normal to shoot with both eyes open because binocular vision allows us to judge ranges and monocular vision does not. There are, however, shooting men who always prefer to shoot with their left eyes closed and sometimes this may be advisable, with reservations. For instance, you may find that you have reasonable success when shooting birds in front, overhead or to the right, but

that birds coming in on the left are frequently missed. This could be because, whereas your right eye is normally the master eye, the bird suddenly appearing to the left is picked up first by your left eye, and that this eye 'holds on to' it, directs the muzzles to the wrong place and causes a miss. Such apparently inexplicable misses to the left are not very common but if you do find such a thing happening it is worth consulting a coach at a shooting school and he will soon diagnose the cause of the trouble. The misses may have nothing to do with eyesight but if they are caused by the left eye taking control there is no remedy in the fit and shape of the gun. The only solution is to dim, or half close the left eye, not when the bird is first seen, but as the muzzles are put on to it so that the right eye takes over as the gun is mounted. Partially closing the left eye is sufficient and a complete wink, which might be a bit of a strain, is not necessary. The dimming of the left eye can take place at any time after binocular vision is no longer required, which means after the bird has been recognized and its range and course appreciated, and usually the shooter finds it convenient to concentrate his viewing through his right eye about half-way through mounting his gun.

When both eyes are equally strong the gun must have a central vision fitting which entails considerable cast-off so that the rib appears centrally in front of both eyes. (Photograph 2).

Even with a normal right master-eye it may be necessary to check the fit of a gun as its owner becomes older. Young men see out of the centre of the pupil but with middle age there comes an increasing tendency to look out of the inner corner of the eye; the slight displacement of the start of the line of sight means that the barrels are pushed over to the left but the shooter is not aware of how, or why, he misses on that side, only that he does. A visit to a shooting school, where the instructor can check alignment of eye and muzzles, can correct this fault by using the try-gun to check cast-off, which will have to be increased. With a little extra cast-off the effects of age can be reduced.

If the left eye is definitely master or if the right has lost its sight there is no reason why shooting should not be done from the left

18 **The left eye taking control**   This young shot, before he went to a Shooting School, was unaware that his left eye often took control. This picture proves the point, for the eye looks at the camera while the gun points to the side

19 The left eye A dimmed, half-closed left eye, as advocated under certain circumstances in Chapter 4. The finger is on the trigger of the second barrel and the loader has his left hand up ready to take the empty gun

20 Dimming the left eye Dimming the left eye again. It is practised more often than many people realize, and is certainly helpful if there is any doubt about which eye is master

shoulder, except that it may be awkward for the normally right handed man. To shoot from the right shoulder, using the left eye, an across-eyed stock is required; this makes an odd-looking gun which has much exaggerated cast-off but it is a good arrangement for a man who has lost his right eye. In a case where the left eye is master but the right is perfectly good if it could be made to work, an across-eyed stock is not worth the trouble, and the better solution is to half close the left eye as the gun is mounted, as described above.

An eye guard can be fitted on the barrels to block the vision of a left master-eye and it will be satisfactory for low shots but not much use for high ones because the blotting out of the left eye's vision is left until too late. The guard is really only worth while if the shooter is physically incapable of learning to close his left eye.

If you have faulty vision which requires spectacles to correct it you may find it advisable to have a special pair for shooting. These should have large lenses, with a shape like a triangle with rounded corners, to give you a good field of view and they can also with advantage have the lower edge of the lenses set a little further away from the face than normal; this will help to keep the line of sight more nearly at right angles through the lenses when you are looking upwards.

As a final comment on gun mounting, you are recommended to try to cultivate a good style. Watch good shots in action and you you will see perfect balance, unhurried movements, rhythm and swing and a certain snap as the shot is actually taken; watching such a performance you will feel convinced that the shot has connected with the target without bothering to look and see, but, of course, you must watch the man on the ground and not be tempted to stare upwards to see the pheasants tumbling out of the sky. Style cannot be perfect every time for, just as the greatest cricket batsmen make mistakes occasionally, so do the expert shots sometimes fail to shoot straight. But when your style *is* right you can feel it; you know your gun muzzles are right on the line of flight of the bird, you know just when to pull the trigger and you are so certain of a kill that there is no need to look and see. And the secret of good style is practice in gun mounting.

5 The going-away shot and the approacher

The going-away shot may be the straightforward one flying directly from the shooter at about shoulder height, or it may be ascending or descending or it may be veering slightly to one side or the other.

For the walked-up bird going straight away the first essential is that the shooter should stop walking and adopt a steady stance before he tries to put up his gun; you must not bring up the gun as the left foot comes to the ground and still less must you try to shoot with the right foot in front. Place your left foot firmly on the ground towards the bird, which is at 12 o'clock, with the toes pointing at about one o'clock, body leaning forward slightly so that most of the weight is on that leg; the right foot is about eight inches behind the left, toes pointing at about 3 o'clock, heel just off the ground. Now, with the left hand put the gun muzzles right at the bird so that you look through and past the end of the barrels at the bird *before* you start to mount the butt; the gun is held out slightly in front of you, muzzles up, butt down and you are watching the flight of the bird and keeping the muzzles precisely in the line between your eye and the bird. Push the safety catch off and mount the butt quietly and smoothly to the shoulder and cheek, still holding the muzzles firmly on the bird; press the trigger as the gun is locked into shoulder and cheek. There should be no hurry about this movement of raising the butt and firing, it must all be done with rhythm and smoothness but, of course, without any waiting about which would allow the bird to fly out of range. If you have started early enough, having seen the bird in range, you ought to be able to stop, put your muzzles on, bring up the butt and fire in about $1\frac{1}{2}$ seconds. Remember, incidentally, not to snatch

---

21 **Ready** Waiting. The beaters can be heard approaching and the Gun stands up and is ready for the birds. Dog and loader are also alert and watching

22 Seen from the target
Bird's eye view of the line
from the shooter's eye, past
the end of the barrels, to the
target

23 Preparation for the shot
The shooter prepares for his shot by
lining up the muzzles between his
eye and the bird

at the trigger. A shotgun trigger should be squeezed smoothly in the same way as a rifle's, except that there are no first and second pressures. The word 'pull' is frequently used in referring to pressing the trigger but this must not be misconstrued into meaning any sort of jerkiness. (Study Photographs 22 to 25).

It is most important to start every shot correctly and, in fact, once you have got your muzzle fairly on the bird, with the butt still down, you have done 75 per cent of the job; bringing up the butt and pulling the trigger is then easy and unhurried. If you watch a good shot in action you will see at once the deliberate, smooth motion with which he moves his gun and this is the only way to shoot properly. Jerky movements inevitably cause misses because the muzzle is waved around and loses the target. This instruction is meant to get you to put your muzzle on the target and hold it like a radar set clamping on to an aircraft, and never let it go until after the shot has been fired.

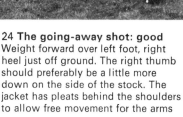

24 The going-away shot: good
Weight forward over left foot, right heel just off ground. The right thumb should preferably be a little more down on the side of the stock. The jacket has pleats behind the shoulders to allow free movement for the arms

25 The going-away shot: bad Weight back on right foot, body turned too much to front, left hand too far back, fingers over top of barrels, left elbow down in rifle shooting manner

Let us now consider a bird which, instead of going straight away from us, veers to one side a bit. It is going away at an angle, to your left, so what do you do? Start off exactly as before; firm stance, with the feet, keep your eye on the bird and put your muzzles on it, only this time the muzzles move up behind the bird and pass along through it as the butt comes up to the shoulder. As the muzzles pass the bird's beak you pull the trigger and you continue swinging on and you keep your cheek glued to the stock. The muzzles in this case made a slight movement to the left whereas in the previous shot they merely came straight up until the bird was blotted out. You knew this second bird was going to the left because you saw its head on that side; this is most important as a good many easy going-away shots are missed because the shooter fails to realize that the bird is not going quite straight away but at a slight angle. Watch for the bird's head and you will be sure which way it is flying.

26 Bird approaching on right First position for a bird approaching on the right. Muzzle on the bird, eye looking past the end of the barrels at the target. Weight leaning forward, forefinger on the trigger guard, thumb pushing safely catch forward. The line Eye-Muzzle -Target is indicated. This is correct preparation for the shot

27 Bird approaching on right Second position, muzzle still held on line of flight of the bird, body pivoting round to right, forefinger moving towards trigger

'Cheek glued to the stock' said the instructor, for how often has he seen a pupil lift his cheek off in order to see the effect of the shot? Everyone does it at sometime or other and it is nearly always fatal because, although you may intend only to lift the cheek slightly *after* you have fired, the chances are 10 to 1, or maybe 100 to 1, that you will raise the cheek before or as you fire, and then the line Eye – Muzzle – Target is broken and the result is a miss.

While taking this shot, and also the straight-away one, lean more and more forward, pushing your gun after the bird, your right heel rising off the ground. This keeps you flexible, helps to smooth out your movements and lessens the likelihood of your adopting a rigid posture which would be certain to kill your swing

28 **Bird approaching on right**
Third position, the moment of firing;
shoulder forward to butt, left arm
reaching well up, body pivoted
further round to right, left knee
braced, right heel raised off ground.
The left forefinger might well be a
little straighter, along the line of the
barrels

29 **Bird approaching on
right** The wrong way.
Stance too wide, weight
mostly on the right foot, gun
canted over clockwise, cheek
away from the stock, body
leaning over to the right. The
dog has become bored;
perhaps he knows the shot is
going to be another miss

stone dead. You must never lean back but it is particularly important with this shot to be leaning forward because, if you are upright for the first shot, the recoil from the more or less horizontal
gun will push you back and you will be trying to fire the second
barrel from a stiff and awkward position with the weight on the
wrong foot.

The bird going away but a bit to the right requires the same
technique as the one going to the left, but for most shooters it is a
slightly more difficult shot because of the comparative awkward-
ness of swinging the left arm across the body. Here the forward
lean will help again. Try standing incorrectly, with the weight back
on the right foot, and then swing your gun slowly across your front

to the right. There will be a perceptible tendency for the gun to cant over clockwise and this in shooting means the shot going low. So concentrate on the lean forward, weight on the left foot, toes pointing towards the bird, and body and arms loose and flexible, never tensed. In fact, the left arm should not swing across the body at all, since the turn to the right should be made by pivoting from the hips. The tendency for the left arm to swing across the body arises from having the trunk of the body tensed instead of relaxed.

If a bird is ascending as it goes away you must swing your gun up and through it but there is often a tendency here to shoot too soon, particularly at a pheasant which suddenly jumps up at one's feet, calling in alarm and surprising the shooter by its sudden appearance. This target is astonishingly easy to miss, and probably with both barrels too, the shot going harmlessly under the bird's tail. The acceleration of the bird as it jumps into the air is very fast but if you watch it you will very likely see that when it has reached 10 or 20 feet up it flies away and perhaps descends a little, or even if it flies straight, its path apparent to the gun is one of descent. Therefore, when the bird first appears do not hurry; place your muzzle on it, watch its flight and when it has settled down keep the muzzle tight on the target which you will see is moving slightly downwards, bring up the butt, keep the muzzle swinging and pull. You will then achieve an easy shot at 20 or 30 yards instead of missing what you thought was an easy one only a few feet in front of you. Take your time and watch the flight; again, with the muzzle kept steadily on the target you have achieved 75 per cent of your task before ever you mount the gun to your shoulder.

With a more gently ascending bird going away the muzzle is swung up and through the bird and the shot taken as the bird is blotted out. The rate of swing depends on the angle of ascent and how far away the target is. For instance, a bird twenty yards out rising to clear a hedge requires a quick swing to catch him before he goes out of sight; this is a fairly simple shot. But if the same bird is forty yards away his rate of ascent appears to be slower, your swing will be correspondingly slower and conscious effort needs to be made to keep the swing going on upwards so as not to miss behind.

Now for the low approaching bird coming straight in: pick it up in the same way, same stance and still pushing your gun well forward. Although the bird is coming at you its apparent path is slightly ascending and you must shoot a little in front of it. So you pick the bird up with the muzzle, only this time first at its feet and then move up its body until it is blotted out by the barrels. Only a very small movement of the gun is required and you can shoot as soon as you lose sight of your target. No jerkiness must be allowed, smoothness and rhythm being required always. The point particularly to guard against is swaying back on your heels because the mere fact of the bird coming at you tends to make you subconsciously lean back instead of remembering the all-important virtue of leaning forward.

With the same bird quartering in to you from either side the method of shooting is similar to when the bird was quartering away. Pick it up behind its tail and swing through, but remember a good rule here which is to keep inside the course of the bird: for a bird coming in from the left the muzzle should start behind its tail and pass over the tip of its left wing, and if the bird is coming in from the right the muzzle should swing through the tip of its right wing. In this way the swing is more likely to follow the true path of the bird since a more direct swing, trying to follow the body of the bird, will probably result in the shot going outside its flight line and missing. Again you must be careful not to sway back and any turning motion must be a pivot directly from the hips.

You may meet a descending approaching bird, as in the case of a pigeon coming down to some decoys. The drill is again to put the muzzle on and to accentuate its downward movement as the butt comes up. It can be an awkward shot and you must concentrate on getting the butt properly home to your shoulder and your cheek well onto the stock. The swing should be rapid and well through the bird's beak since its downward movement is probably more than you appreciate.

The bird going down and away from you is sometimes a difficult shot, and this state of affairs can occur in a grouse butt with the hill dropping away from you. Whether you have missed in front or killed one bird and then wish to deal with this fellow behind, you must take the gun completely off your shoulder and keep the barrels up. Then turn round, find a good stance, just as you did when walking-up before you attempted to fire, and as you are settling your feet keep the gun held out in front of you with the muzzle on the bird. Push the muzzle out, down along the line of flight, lean forward and swing through just underneath the bird. This is about the only occasion when you are permitted to see the bird just over your barrels as you pass it, for it is going down and you must ensure that the gun keeps swinging down too. In most other cases, as for instance in a highish crossing shot in front, the exhortation will be to imagine you are brushing the muzzle through the bird's back feathers, so ensuring that the shot is kept well up. For a grouse skimming downhill, however, your problem is to make sure you do not shoot over him.

In the quartering shot going away you were told to watch for the bird's head as an indication of whether the target really was moving off to one side and not simply directly away. In amplification of this it is a sound rule, but difficult to observe, that the shooter should *always* look at only the head of the bird or beast he is trying to shoot. A pheasant's long tail is one of its best protections, for the untrained human eye is drawn to it and many misses must be put down to the instinctive feeling that here is a great, long target, too easy to miss, we can shoot as soon as we get on to it, and the result: the gun had never even reached the real target, the head, when the decision to pull the trigger was made, so the bird departs with no more than the loss of the odd tail feather. With a hare the same problem arises and it really is difficult to make yourself look at its head and not at that long body. Geese, too, are missed because they look so big and yet they obligingly stick their necks out and show the target, the head, well in front, as do duck. Temperament affects the individual shooter in his ability to concentrate on the head of a bird, and the excitable fellow will always look quickly at the whole body, swing up his gun, fire and usually miss. The good shot must be naturally steady and phlegmatic or else he must train himself so to be. If you find difficulty in keeping your eye on the head of your birds practise when you are not shooting; on a country walk make yourself lock your eyes on to the heads of birds you see, be they pigeon or starlings, plovers, gulls or game birds. Disregard the markings on their bodies, their tails, legs, the flapping of their wings and think only of their heads. And when you are shooting say to yourself as a bird appears: 'Its head . . . head . . . head!' And more than likely, when you have fired that bird will be dead, dead, dead. . . .

If you are starting shooting, or if you have shot before by the light of nature and are now trying to learn how to do it properly, do not be disheartened by the number of things you are told to do all in the very short space of time between seeing a bird and firing at it. It is easy to concentrate on having your feet right and then forget about your left hand putting the muzzle on the target, or perhaps to get those two right and then omit to keep your cheek hugging the stock. But it is all much the same as learning to drive a car: at first there seem to be just too many things to do at once when you have to change gear, but after a while it comes naturally and as you become more experienced, it is practically automatic and can be done almost without conscious thought. So it is with shooting; but you *must* learn the right sequence, memorize it and then practise and practise until all the movements happen naturally and automatically.

From these first shots, starting with the simplest going-away one, we can list a sequence of actions for all shots, as follows:

Gun ready – loaded, muzzle held down.
See the bird ⎤ and decide that if it holds its
Identify it ⎦ course you may shoot at it.
Estimate range – (see page 33).
Settle stance – move left foot if necessary, pivot on right toe.
Aim – butt still down but muzzle on target.
Swing – pivoting from the hips.
Mount gun – shoulder to stock.
Fire – squeeze the trigger.
Continue swing – no check after firing.
Assess result – fire second barrel if required.
Cheek off stock – but not before this.
Gun down.
Reload.

Study Photographs 26 to 28 and 30 to 32.

The approaching and going-away shots explained in this chapter are generally fairly easy ones and you ought to kill most of the birds you meet in these circumstances. There are, however, several more difficult shots and, as well as the type of shot, the species of bird can make the shooting more or less difficult; similarly, with game birds all the shooting is easier at the beginning of the season than it is later on. These points should be considered when discussion arises, and personal claims are made, about the number of cartridges expended compared with the number of birds killed.

A high average of kills to cartridges can be obtained by choosing only the easier shots and when game is plentiful, as on a good pheasant shoot, this is not too difficult. Perhaps it is done more

30 *(Above left)* **A bird to the left**   A lady-shot demonstrates a bird taken slightly behind as it flies to her left. Here she is in the ready position, watching the bird with the muzzle on it. Left forefinger along the underneath of the barrels, right forefinger along trigger guard. The weight is well forward over the left foot but the right leg is perhaps a little stiff

31 *(Above Right)* **A bird to the left**   The muzzles are following the line of flight of the bird to the left, the body pivots from the hips. Presumably the shot has not already been taken because the bird was previously out of range or it may have been partly concealed from view by trees. Note that the right heel is rising slightly off the ground.

32 *(Opposite)* **A bird to the left**   The shot has just been taken. The body has pivoted well round on the hips, weight on left leg, right heel raised. Note left thumb, straight along side of barrel

often than it should be. A low average will result from shooting away at everything, and this is stupid and unsporting because many of the birds shot at ought to have been left for another Gun and others were out of range anyway. It is very difficult to keep an accurate count of cartridges and kills unless you have a scorer, as is done sometimes on big shoots in Europe. It is not uncommon for the Gun who thinks he has acquitted himself well at an English pheasant stand to say afterwards to his loader: 'Didn't do too badly that time. Reckon I only let through two or three birds!' Or, if he is a little more modest, or truthful, he may claim: 'I think I got every other bird, at least.' But the loader, or the keeper or the man with the dogs who is picking-up may have a look on the

ground and count up thirty empty cartridge cases. He knows only ten birds were brought down by that gun, but he is not surprised. He has heard such claims many times before.

The good shot takes every bird that is his and in range and he misses more than he kills. So do not be downhearted when you miss.

At certain stands at driven game a good shot may well shoot nearly as many birds as he uses cartridges, but over the whole season his average is likely to be one kill in three shots. Very high averages may be made when shooting pigeon that are coming in well to decoys; 200 cartridges and 170 pigeon is quite possible. An afternoon on the marsh after snipe, however, can lower the season's average and humble the shooter, who may well miss a dozen in a row. Two reports of exceptional pigeon shooting appeared in the shooting press in the same year; one was of a highly skilled gentleman who killed 550 pigeon in a day, between about eleven o'clock and four o'clock, and the other concerned the altruistic confession of a somewhat different shot who expended 250 cartridges and only managed to kill three birds. Both performances must have affected the shooters' averages.

Most shooting men, because of the restricted type of shooting which they are able to do, tend to become good at certain shots of which they have considerable experience and indifferent at other shots not necessarily more difficult. You may see a man put up a superb performance at high pheasants and then, during a lull in proceedings, miss with both barrels a magpie drifting along at hedge height. Some men hate shooting hares, largely because they know they rarely hit the animals in the head and they dislike merely wounding them in the back legs. The game shot who primarily shoots pheasants is sometimes a poor performer at pigeon, often because pheasants fly fairly straight whereas pigeon nearly always jink.

Nobody likes to miss but when you do, take heart by remembering that others also fail, quite frequently. One kill to two cartridges throughout a day is good shooting but one in three is more likely; one in four is quite satisfactory for the average shot. The first class shot, of whom there are remarkably few, probably averages about seventy kills to a hundred cartridges during a season of shooting driven pheasants; if he enjoys snipe shooting and wildfowling, etc., as well his average is unlikely to be over 50 per cent.

6 The crossing shot

This shot will be considered in two main divisions, the horizontal crosser and the vertical crosser.

The horizontal crosser to the left should be a fairly easy shot. Imagine you are standing waiting for the birds to be driven towards you, and you are on the left of the line of Guns; a pheasant flies low out of the wood in front of you and hurries off to your left, 20 yards or so away and only about 20 feet up. Your weight is on your left foot, you put the gun muzzles on the bird, pivot your body round to the left push forward the safety catch, swing through the bird from his tail out to his beak as the stock comes up, and as the shoulder meets the butt you fire. If you do this fairly quickly, and *look* at the bird's head and not at its tail, it is practically certain that your shot will be a kill. Had that shot been a crosser to the right you would not have taken it because the bird was too low for the safety of the Guns on your right, but in safe conditions your method of taking the shot would have been the same as for the one to the left, remembering especially to keep your weight forward and on your left foot, to pivot fully from the hips and not to sway over on to your right foot.

'What about aiming in front?' you may ask. 'Don't I have to give a forward allowance for these shots?' – And here we must discuss allowance, or lead as it is sometimes called, and swing or what some people describe as overthrow.

Tables of allowances for birds crossing at various speeds and ranges have been calculated but they are of no practical value to the modern game shot. Judgement of distance, especially aerial distance, is difficult and it varies between individuals, as does mental reaction time which governs the delay between the brain deciding to fire and the finger actually pulling the trigger. These theoretical allowances tell us how far in front of a bird we need to point the gun, and the distances are considerable, as, for instance,

8 feet for a driven partridge or pheasant at 40 yards. You, how-ever, will not bother yourself with any measured distance of lead in front of your targets because you will shoot with a swinging gun, and this will throw the shot in front of the bird's position at the moment of firing so that shot and bird meet at a point in space some distance ahead.

When shooting at a close, fast-moving bird, such as the pheas-ant we considered just now, the swing of the gun is quick and the necessary overthrow of the shot is applied almost automatically and probably subconsciously. With a small bird like a teal or partridge the shot is likely to be even more certain of success because the impression of speed is greater and there is no long tail to distract the shooter's eye. These close, fast-crossing shots are genuinely easy and as long as the gun is mounted properly very little can go wrong. But the slow, so called, 'easy' crossers and the longer-range ones are often missed, nearly always behind.

No more forward movement of the gun is needed to shoot the correct distance ahead of a bird at 40 yards than for one at 20 yards, the angular displacement being the same. (See Figure 3.) But the important point to realize is, that as the range increases, the movement of the gun, following the line of flight of the bird, slows down.

The *apparent* speed of the bird is less at longer ranges and it governs the speed at which the gun is swung, and so something must be done to counteract this slower gun movement. The further the bird is away the greater will be the effect of only a small muzzle movement ahead but it is also more difficult to accelerate the swing and to make it continue past the target. For this reason you must give some forward allowance at long range and you must do it consciously.

The amount of forward allowance is a picture in the shooter's eye and *not* a specific number of feet, and only experience can build up a series of such pictures for various angles of shots at different ranges. An oblique, quartering shot for example, needs less lead than a direct horizontal crosser, which needs the most. As examples of these 'individual pictures', consider the cases of two good shots who visited a shooting school because they had found that they often missed longish crossing birds. Each fired several times at crossing clay-pigeons and at first they missed behind, as the instructor could see. After he had been told to swing further and further ahead one of the Guns began to break the clays, and

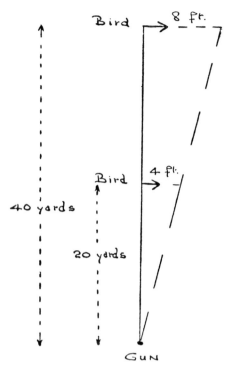

Figure 3 Diagram to show that, theoretically, the angular forward allowance for a bird crossing at 20 yards is the same as for one crossing at the same speed at 40 yards, assuming that shot speed is constant

he then said 'That's it! Now I've got the idea, and I can go on hitting them.' And he did, for several more shots. He was then asked how much forward allowance he found it necessary to give those long range crossers and he replied 'Ah, I know exactly now. It's a good ten feet.'

The other visitor to the school who had begun by missing behind was also brought on target by his instructor, and he too expressed satisfaction and declared that he had found out exactly how to deal with that particular shot. When asked what allowance he gave to obtain kills his reply was: 'All this stuff about eight feet or more is nonsense. I reckon I'm right on them when I give nine inches.'

The inference from these examples is that both shooters were right in their description of their personal pictures of the target at the moment of pulling the trigger. These pictures can only be acquired by the individual from trial, and correction and experience. You may hear someone talking about 'giving him a gate' when describing how he brought off a long shot and he means that his forward allowance, by his reckoning, was 10 feet or so but that does not mean that you, in the same circumstances, would try and give the same 'gate' by your reckoning. If you miss long-range crossers, 35 to 40 yards, not abnormally long-range ones, and you know your stance was correct and your gun mounting was smooth and sure, you can assume that the misses were behind. So you must adjust your picture: open it out, keep swinging further ahead, increasing at each shot until you have success. Make yourself hold on to the swing well after the shot has left your gun barrels and ensure that you do not take your cheek off the stock to see the result.

Remember that the slower the swing, because of the slow, or apparently slow, speed of the target the more you must consciously prolong it to give the forward allowance. Those 'easy' close-range crossing shots are missed because of a slow swing ending in the gun being halted as it is fired; if a hare dashes past you the odds are that you will fling up your gun, swing, pull, 'Bang!' and the hare somersaults to a standstill. But if it lollops along unconcernedly, listening to the beaters behind but unaware of you standing still in front of it, you will find it all too easy to move your gun slowly up to the animal, check as you pull and miss an absurdly 'easy' shot at 15 yards. A very strong conscious effort of will, a firm determination and the confidence that such is the correct action is required to make yourself swing ahead under these conditions. Do not, on any crossing shot when you know you are going to give a forward lead, try to mount the gun, and then swing past your target. The swing must start with a body pivot from the hips as the gun is being mounted, and continue on as butt and shoulder meet.

You were told on page 74 to look at the heads of your targets and to disregard the size of their bodies. This is especially important in the case of crossing shots and when considering forward allowance, because your picture of this allowance must be from a bird's beak and not from the middle of its body. You may learn a little from the story of the young lad who was taken on his first duck shoot by his father. 'You must hit them in the head only,' said Father. 'Mallard are tough and the shot will only bounce off their body feathers.' So young George concentrated on the heads of the duck, and he killed several. After the shoot he was given two birds to take home and when he plucked them he found several pellets in the bodies. He took them to Father to show how wrong was the belief that the body feathers would deflect shot, but the wise parent told him: 'George, if you had shot *at* the ducks' bodies all those pellets would not have hit at all. They would have missed behind.' George profited from the lesson, taught himself always to look at only the heads of birds, and today he is a first-class shot.

The overhead crosser poses different problems from the horizontal one and the most obvious is that with the overhead shot the bird is out of sight behind the gun barrels at the moment of firing whereas the lower bird can be kept in view nearly all the time. Imagine a pheasant flying over the trees in front of you, on a course that will take it straight over your head. Immediately you lean forward on the left leg, toes at about 1 o'clock and right foot pointing at about 3 o'clock, put the muzzles on the bird's flight, line, starting behind its tail although you are looking at its head, and slide the safety catch forward; then raise the muzzles up through the bird, bring the stock up without altering the position of your head as you look up naturally, and reach up with your body and arm as if you were trying to brush that pheasant out of the sky. Keep your leg stiff and raise your right heel. Let the gun muzzles pass the bird's head and fire as you lose sight of it. Provided that you kept the swing going you should hear a satisfying thump behind you **as** the bird hits the ground. This vertical swing is most elegant **when** properly performed but it is not a difficult gymnastic exercise; it does, however, need practice in order to make the arms and shoulders move freely so that there is no check towards the top of the swing. You should also take care to avoid any tendency to sway your weight back on to your right foot, because, although this may seem an obvious and easily adopted position, the transference of the weight completely blocks your swing; as the weight goes back you will find that the swing comes to a stop and it can only be continued by a determined jerk which spoils the rhythm and is unlikely to lead to success. Your head should not be tipped back for a vertical shot except in conjunction with the bending movement of your body; it is wrong to bend the neck backwards as you strain to look upwards. In fact, in all shots your head should remain in the same, natural, looking-ahead position in relation to your body; if you want to shoot downwards, as at a rabbit, your body should bend forwards from

33 The overhead shot
Waiting for pheasants to appear over the trees

34 The overhead shot A bird appears and the shooter puts his muzzles on it, safety catch off, finger along trigger guard, weight on left foot

the hips and when you shoot upwards your body should bend back, but your neck must never be cricked down into a chin-on-chest attitude nor bent back with your chin stuck up into the air (Photographs 33 to 37).

Another problem with the overhead crosser as compared with the horizontal one is the greater difficulty of judging range in the sky than nearer the ground, where objects other than the target help the shooter to decide the range. Hence the need to learn what birds look like at different ranges, as mentioned on page 33. You need to know approximately how high your vertical crosser is in order to vary your forward allowance; with a low bird you can fire as the muzzles pass its head and with a high one you must consciously speed up the swing and make sure that the muzzles are well past the target before you shoot. High pheasants are discussed in greater detail on pages 117–120.

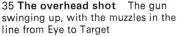

35 **The overhead shot** The gun swinging up, with the muzzles in the line from Eye to Target

36 **The overhead shot** The moment of firing. Reaching out and up, weight forward, right heel raised slightly. An excellent position

Many shots, of course, are not direct vertical or horizontal crossers, but oblique ones and, while gun mounting remains the same for these, your eye has to estimate the degree of obliqueness and so decide the amount of lead required. The golden rule to remember is that misses are nearly always below and behind. Study Figure 1 (page 32) again. In fact, you can take it as certain that your missed shots are low and behind unless there is something definitely wrong with your eyesight or the fit of your gun. One of the unfortunate results of poor shooting at pheasants is the sight of a bird flying towards shelter with a leg hanging down; this shows that it has been hit back and under the tail because that is where the legs are carried in flight. Such a distressing situation can become too common when the shooting is of a low standard and it emphasizes the need for a team of men with dogs to stand behind the guns and pick up the birds, particularly watching

out for wounded ones. No organized shoot is complete without one or two dogmen to do the picking-up. Apart from the aspect of avoiding unnecessary suffering by the birds, the use of pickers-up increases the bag, even when some of the Guns have their own dogs.

Imagine that you are taking a shot at a pheasant rising and crossing obliquely to your right. You put the gun up at it, pivoting from your hips, and the muzzles pass the bird's tail; you swing on and, as the target is about 30 yards away, you get your 'picture' right to give the appropriate amount of allowance and you fire, and miss. Why? Because the shot went below and behind.

The oft-repeated teaching for this oblique shot is to imagine that your gun barrels are 'brushing the bird's feathers the wrong way along its back'. The muzzles should pass over the back of the bird and across its nape, and the shot is taken over the top of its head, or beyond this point if more forward allowance is needed. Sometimes it may be obvious that the bird is rising as well as crossing and you will naturally try to take into account the gain in height, but at other times, as for instance when a bird flies out from above the trees, your eye is watching the bird in the sky and may easily register it as simply a crossing shot, whereas it really is rising as well. Pheasants rarely fly straight as far as altitude is concerned; they nearly always rise up and then plane down. Unless it is patently obvious that your bird is descending you can assume that it is rising; you must remind yourself that it is and adopt the habit of brushing the feathers up its back. Two reasons for missing this shot are taking the cheek off the stock too soon and not being confident of shooting with the first aim; you should by now realize the extreme importance of always resisting the temptation to raise your cheek off the stock as you fire; you must also appreciate that your first aim has an instinctive accuracy, and that if you hang on to your shot and push your gun across the sky, wondering if you have placed it above the bird's neck, your swing will slow down and cause you to miss behind.

The importance of relying on your first aim is brought to the fore in any shot when your gun barrels pass over or through the target just before you fire. That is the time when you may feel doubtful whether you really are on the correct line of the bird, and

37 **The overhead shot**   A bad position. Weight back on right foot, left heel raised and a heavy grip with the left hand

if you falter you are lost. Remember the expert shot's style: an unhurried but steady mounting of the gun and a snap at the finish, with the trigger squeezed as the shoulder comes to the butt. There is also a tendency to lose faith in first aim when trying to 'make sure' of a shot. Perhaps is is the first bird of the day, or a 'gallery shot' when the other Guns are watching, or it could be simply a shot at a bird that you particularly want to take home for dinner after a casual walk round on a rough shoot. If you think to yourself, 'I *must* get this one,' you will almost certainly slow your swing, poke at the bird and miss. 'Making sure' is fatal.

The opposite of trying to make too sure of a shot is a light-hearted and optimistic attitude which allows you to think, 'Of course I'll get this one.' This is much more satisfactory and should lead to a state when you can say for *certain* that a shot is going to be a kill as you press the trigger. When you know you have picked up a bird correctly over the muzzles, that your stance is correct and your swing smoothly flowing, you will gain such confidence that you feel you could close both eyes as you fire and know you have scored a kill. Indifferent shots have said that they would open another eye if they had it, and they would doubtless express alarm if it was suggested that they might close their eyes instead; closing the eyes is not, of course, advocated but the feeling of confidence that one could do so is to be encouraged, because it shows that the shot has been taken correctly from beginning to end. And with confidence comes better shooting.

There are other minor factors affecting these crossing shots and three of them concern the shot in your cartridges; they *are* only minor factors, their effect being measurable merely in inches, and they apply to long ranges but are of no importance at short range. The speed of shot decreases with range and therefore Figure 3 is not strictly true in practice, since it would only apply if the shot speed was constant. The effect of the falling speed of the shot is that the gun should be pointed a little further ahead at long range than at short range, but the amount is so small compared with the distance measurable in feet of many misses behind the target that it may be ignored, except to remind us once again to swing well in front at long range, for we are unlikely to miss ahead and all too likely to do so astern.

Gravity causes shot to drop and at long range this will bring the gun's pattern down a little. In fact, from a gun fired horizontally, the centre of the shot pattern drops only about 3 inches at 40 yards. As the effect of dropping shot is so small it should give no cause for worry, but it does emphasize the value of sweeping the gun along the top of the target, brushing a bird's back feathers, and taking care not to swing along its belly which would surely result in a miss below. Do not, however, try to use the fact that shot drops as an excuse for missing; regard it merely as source of confidence in the fact that if you keep your swing well up you will hit your target and not shoot over the top of it.

The third element in the behaviour of shot which we should now consider is the fact that the pattern has depth as well as breadth. When you look at the pellet marks on a pattern plate you are tempted to visualize the shot in the air forming a similar flat pattern, whereas the shot charge spreads lengthways on leaving the gun, as well as sideways. The shot forms a column which, at 35 yards, is about 7 feet long, and this provides a shotgun user with a margin of error, provided he keeps ahead of his target. A 100 per cent hit places the target in the middle of the 30-inch circle of shot pattern, but naturally this does not happen very often; usually the target is somewhere in the circle and it may even be partly outside it and still be sufficiently hit by the pattern to be killed. If the leading edge of the circle is just at the back of a bird all the pellets will miss behind, but if the circle is slightly ahead of the bird the later pellets in the column of shot will meet the bird as it moves forward and they may very well be sufficient to obtain a kill. The formation of the shot into a pattern of depth is called shot 'stringing' and with good cartridges the length of the shot string is of no consequence at short ranges; it does not make much difference to shooting even at longer ranges, because the speed of the shot approaching a crossing bird at right angles is much greater than the bird's speed, so that the bird does not move very far forward in the time taken for the shot string to pass it.

Example: The shot column at 35 yards is about 7 feet.
The shot takes about 1/10 second to travel 35 yards.
A bird crossing at 30 m.p.h. travels $4\frac{1}{2}$ feet in 1/10 second.
To travel 7 feet (length of shot column)
   shot takes $1/10 \times 7/105$ (105 is 35 yards in feet).

$$= \frac{7}{1050} \text{ second.}$$

How far will the bird fly in 7/1050 second?

In 1/10 second it moves 54 inches (4½ feet).

So in 7/1050 second it moves $\dfrac{54 \times 7}{105} = 3.6$.

The answer to the question, 'How far does the bird advance while the shot string passes it?' is therefore, 'About 3½ inches.'

The useful feature of shot stringing is that it makes a miss in front more difficult. If you swing a bit too far ahead of your bird, there is a chance that it may fly into the main body of the shot pattern, whereas if your forward allowance is too small the whole of the shot charge must pass behind the bird; it may even hit another bird following a similar line. If this happens to you, profit by the lesson and resolve to open out your picture and swing further ahead when you meet the same conditions again.

Judging distances correctly is of especial importance with crossing shots because, not only do you need to have a good idea of how far away is your target in order to decide whether it is in range of the gun, but on your estimation of its distance away depends how much forward allowance is required. There is no question of thinking to yourself, '40 yards out, give it 8 feet,' but your eye must quickly register a range in order to call up in your mind the correct picture, to be translated into lead as your gun swings through the target. Make yourself practice estimating ranges and checking them, as described on page 33, and remember to note the appearance of birds at various known distances.

Shooting in a strong wind is never easy and such conditions can upset good and experienced shooters. The effect of the wind on the shot is negligible in practice, but its effect on the birds may be considerable. Obviously, birds going downwind will be faster and you will need to open out your picture on the crossers and give them more lead. Probably after a few experimental shots you will find these fast flyers easier than you expected, but the birds going upwind can be more difficult, because your swing will be much slower and may develop into a poke. A bird 20 yards away, flapping past into the wind, almost hovering at times as a pigeon does when it is keeping low in the folds of the ground to avoid the worst of the wind, looks absurdly easy. For this shot you

---

38 Reaching up   Reaching up for an overhead shot at a pheasant clearing the trees. The gun is an under-and-over. Note loader with cartridges ready

should at all costs avoid getting your gun up too soon: wait until the bird has reached the point where you are going to shoot it, then swing up the gun through the bird's tail and pull as you pass its head. Make yourself swing quickly as you would if the target was a close-range and normally flying partridge. You won't, in fact, swing as fast as that but unless you try to, the slow speed of a bird struggling into a wind will mesmerize you into a horrible exhibition of poking.

A bird flying across the wind is blown slightly to the side of its intended course but generally the shooter's eye appreciates this and a normal swing through is sufficient to keep the gun along the true path of the target. High, curling pheasants can present a more difficult problem, and this is discussed on page 120. Suffice it to remember that wind does not affect the shot but that the consequent behaviour of the birds, particularly on high crossing shots, demands careful attention.

Footwork is mentioned from time to time in this instruction, and there is a point about it that concerns these long crossing shots, associated as they are with the idea of high pheasants, and that is a difficulty of adopting a good stance when standing on a slope. At recognized pheasant stands the positions of the Guns are usually much the same on each shooting occasion and where these occur on a slope, as they often do, a flat platform about a couple of yards square ought to be dug out of the side of the hill. If this is not done the Gun is in an awkward position and he cannot adopt the correct stance because if his left foot is in front of his right it must also be higher, and there is a natural tendency for the weight to be taken on the right leg. If you find yourself in this situation you will have to make the best you can of it, by keeping as much forward on the left foot as possible and by raising the right heel. When the slope is steep you may bend your left knee, which, of course, is normally kept braced; such a stance is preferable to one where both feet, in order to keep them level, are side by side across the slope. With a bent left knee and your left foot ahead of the right you can keep your chest diagonally to your front and you have a good chance of swinging right or left without dropping the weight back on to your right foot and missing your birds because of canted barrels. But beware of getting off balance in this position of the bent left knee because that can cause your body to sway and the gun barrels will wave up and down and spoil your swing. There is no complete answer on how to adopt a good stance when standing on a steep slope; you will have to accept the situation, do the best you can and not be too downhearted when you miss. (Photographs 39 to 44 show footwork.)

The correct way to fire the second barrel deserves some explanation, and the first point to be clear about is that if you kill with your first shot and wish to shoot at another bird some distance away you should take the butt off your shoulder first. Do not poke the gun over towards the second bird and hope to get on to its line. The drill should be: butt off the shoulder, muzzles on to the new target, follow its line of flight, bring up the butt again, and fire. If, however, the birds are close together and more or less in line it is permissible to keep the butt at the shoulder while taking the second shot; but you should appreciate that if two birds, close together and one a little further back than the other, are flying in the same direction you have a better chance of accounting for them both if you take the rearmost bird first. You can then swing forward to the bird in front, keeping the butt to your shoulder, and your swing will not be baulked but, in fact, will be assisted and speeded up which will be a help if the birds originally offered a quartering shot which, by the time you got on to the second, became a crossing shot. If you take the leading bird first, which is the more obvious thing to do, there will be a jolt to your swing as you try to get on to the bird further back and your shot is bound to be erratic. It takes courage to make yourself leave the leading bird and go for one further back, but it is the more certain way of scoring a right-and-left when the birds are reasonably close together, as occurs with partridges, grouse and sometimes pheasants when a flush of them gets up at the same time.

If you use your second barrel to have another shot at a bird you missed with the first, try to increase the speed of your swing; this is usually easy and, indeed, natural, and kills with the second barrel usually denote a slow swing and insufficient allowance for the first shot. Remember, once again, not to take your cheek off the stock after the first shot.

Finally, we will consider briefly the speed of birds in flight, this speed having its greatest effect on our shooting when we are dealing with crossing shots. It is worth remembering that a pheasant flying where it wants to go, which is back to its home covert, usually flies faster and with more determination than when it is being pushed out of the place it knows and has to go elsewhere. That is why intelligent driving of reared pheasants can produce

39 Barrels canting This partridge shooter was waiting for birds to come over the hedge, on his left in the picture. Here he swings round on to a bird going behind him on his right; he has wrongly transferred his weight to his right foot and the gun has canted over to the right. The shot went low and the bird was missed. The left-hand grip is also heavy and not to be commended

40 Barrels canting On another bird to his left he swung round and leant back on his right foot. Again the barrels canted and he missed

41 Pivoting practice
Here he tries some pivoting
practice. His front is
indicated by the marked
stick, and he swings to the
right –

42 – and to the left. The
object is to show that it
really is easy to pivot the
body from the hips through
at least a right angle: the
correct way of shooting to
a flank, rather than keeping
the shoulders towards the
front and merely pushing
the arms to one side or
other

43 Stance on a slope   It is difficult to adopt a good stance when standing on a slope, but you need not be as awkward as this. The feet are together, both knees bent, weight back, the left hand is too far back, thumb over the barrel and the barrels are canted. The dog must be an optimist

better, more difficult and more sporting shooting than can be found by haphazardly pushing out wild birds on a rough shoot. It is also worth noting that a gliding bird, particularly a pheasant, is often travelling faster than when its wings are actually flapping.

Small birds in flight give an impression of greater speed than large birds, but nearly always it is the bigger birds which can fly faster, and you will do well to assume that any large bird you shoot at really is going faster than a small one would be. The slow wing flapping of a goose makes it look as if its speed is less than that of a partridge, but this is a completely false impression. It would be pretty safe to say that no ordinary shooter ever missed a goose in front.

44 Stance on a slope A good forward reach and because of the slope it is permissible to bend the left knee

Many remarkable experiments have been made to determine the speeds of various game birds, and a generally accepted figure is that of something approaching 40 mph, in still air when the bird is driven or alarmed. Such figures are of only academic interest, as are the specific distances of forward allowance. You need only reckon that all the birds you shoot at fly fast, particularly when they are crossing at right angles to you. Be determined to swing out in front of them; strive to make a conscious effort to overcome their speed for that is the only way you will avoid missing behind.

7 The ground shot, the sitter, the snap shot and footwork

The target on the ground is most likely to be a hare or a rabbit and the first point to consider about this shot is the increased risk of unintentionally hitting something else; a shot up into the air is unlikely to hurt anyone, although care is still needed, but a shot into the ground can very easily result in someone being hit.

You must realize that shot can ricochet off any hard surface, such as a tree, and that flints in a ploughed field are practically certain to deflect some of the pellets fired at a hare as it runs across that field. Bushes and hedges can conceal picnickers, or lovers, or children or even somebody's dog. The early autumn is a particularly dangerous time when many people, and especially children, wander all over the countryside collecting mushrooms and blackberries. You should always be careful, when shooting at ground targets, not to follow through into a hedge or wood where the effect of the shot cannot be calculated.

Ferreting for rabbits can be good sport but the excitement and the need for quick shooting when the rabbits appear make it also a potentially dangerous one. February hare drives are fraught with danger when inexperienced and over-enthusiastic Guns fire towards the beating line; ground game has a rousing effect on beaters, too, and they are apt to chase after it during a pheasant drive and try to knock it on the head with their sticks.

Try to make it a rule never to shoot at ground targets if there is any doubt about where your pellets will go. A rabbit running along a hedge is better left alone unless you are sure there is nothing the other side. On a pheasant or partridge drive it is nearly always better to let hares come forward, through the line of Guns, and then shoot them behind. This means turning round, with the gun *not* at the shoulder, in a manner described later in this chapter.

But suppose you do want to shoot a hare advancing to you, the method is to let the gun muzzle run down through its back, past its head and out below its front paws; keep the swing going and fire, and you will have a dead hare, shot cleanly in the head. You must not swing your gun up to the approaching animal, for even if you try to stop the gun as it points at the hare's head, unless the hare stops at the critical moment you will certainly miss behind.

When swinging the gun down, your head must go evenly with it, and neither be left behind in a completely upright pose nor dropped down with the eye in an unnaturally low position. Remember to lean well forward on your left leg and if the shot is particularly downwards, as it will be if the ground slopes down in front of you, *bend* forward from the hips.

Hares are unfortunately wounded far too frequently in the shooting field and the two main reasons are that they are shot at too great a range, sometimes with small pellets such as 7s, and they are shot in the back end only. A hare is a large creature, bigger than most things you shoot at, and you must realize that it still looks quite a reasonable target when it is 40 or 50 yards away. If it is approaching you the time to shoot is when you can clearly see its eyes, and not before. If it is going away from you, fire as soon as you can and let your muzzles swing up through its hind legs, over its body and right up to the tips of its ears; keep swinging and the shot will hit the back of its head. You must resist the temptation to let your eye dwell on the large rump, because to do so is all too easy and it can only result in the hare being wounded and limping on, perhaps screaming in that distressing way which upsets all shooting men. Some people, indeed, so dislike the performance of wounded hares that, whenever possible, they avoid shooting them, but this is a defeatist attitude and if you learn how to shoot them properly you should have no fears on this score.

When a hare is crossing your front and going at full speed it presents a large target and it also exposes all the vulnerable parts of its body. The shot ought to be an easy one, and it will be if you make yourself look immediately at the animal's ears, lean well forward, reach out and swing fast and smoothly through the whole length of the body. Because the animal is crossing, and quickly, you should place your left foot not at the hare but approximately where it will be in a second or so when you are going to shoot it. Thus, you are facing your front with your feet in the normal stance, as in Figure 2; a hare appears slightly to your left front

45 Footwork: crossing hare
The shooter sees a hare to his
left front, running across
towards his right

46 He puts his left foot across
to the right and watches the
hare over his gun muzzles

47 The gun comes up as he
swings round and bends forward
from the waist. His stance is
central so that he can swing
further if required

and it is running across to your right; push your gun out in front
of you, put the muzzle on the target with the butt still down, as
you have with all the other shots, and move your left foot about
ten inches across to the right, in front of your right toe, and lean
forward; your hips are still facing the front and so is the gun, and
then, as the hare runs on to the right and you mount the gun, your
swing is comfortable as it comes over your left foot, and it is more
likely to continue on, with no suspicion of a check, than if your
left foot had stayed back in its original position. With the left
foot where it was, or even moved slightly to the left which would
have been pointing it at the target when first seen, your swing will
be going *away* from your natural central position but by placing
your left foot towards where the hare is going you are swinging
into the central position, and you will have plenty of swing available should you need to fire the second barrel.

If the hare crosses to your left the same rule applies and you
move your left foot a little further round to the left, ready to
swing into your target as you shoot. In both cases you pivot on
the ball of the right foot, raise the right heel slightly and lean

forward, reaching out with the left arm and thrusting the right shoulder into the shot. The left foot moves as soon as you have decided on the hare's probable course and it is ahead of the rest of your body and the gun, which are following up as the hare moves across your front. (See Photographs 45 to 47.)

This drill of moving the left foot before the shot is taken so as to be well placed to swing further if the first barrel misses, or if the target changes direction, can be applied to any target and not only to hares; it is a half-way step towards turning completely round, as described in a moment, for either hare or pheasant. Usually, however, the short step across one's front is less necessary in the case of a pheasant because the bird is more likely to fly a fairly straight course.

Ground game is missed behind as often as is game on the wing but there is a common belief that ground shots very often miss over the top as well; they only do so if the shooter stands too upright, without bending at the hips and without leaning forward. Since footwork plays an important part, as it does in all shots, we will consider it now in the shot that is taken behind.

If you are waiting for pheasants outside a covert and a hare comes towards you, prepare for your shot by placing not your muzzles between your eye and the target, but your left forefinger which is lying along and underneath the barrels; you then have the butt down, by your right hip, and the barrels pointing well up into the air, in a safe manner that cannot allow them to be directed towards the Gun to your flank as you turn round. The hare continues to advance but for safety reasons you decide not to shoot it in front; it then sees you and puts on speed, to pass fairly close to you on one side or the other. You watch it closely, keeping your eye on its ears and your left forefinger moving along its path; as the hare passes you, take a pace round and back with your left foot, to right or left as the case may be, and pivoting on the ball of your right foot; hang on to the line of the hare with your left forefinger, pushing the gun out a little, feel for a firm hold with your left foot, lean forward and mount the gun smoothly to your shoulder. As you do so the muzzles will fall into the line which your eye has never left, since they will now be pointing exactly as your forefinger is pointing and as you see those two big ears going away, shoot. Never once has your eye strayed towards the hare's hindquarters and your shot is a certain kill.

The principle of this shot taken behind is to take the pace round to the rear as early as possible in the gun mounting so that you are well poised by the time the butt comes up, and to be looking all the time through the spot where your left hand holds the barrels. Exactly the same manoeuvre is carried out when you need to turn round to take a really low bird, such as might appear when partridges or grouse are being driven. By keeping your finger on the bird the muzzles are held well clear of your neighbouring Guns and you do not lose the bird's line of flight.

After an overhead shot at a bird you may also wish to turn round, either because you missed with the first barrel or to take a second bird which has approached too nearly overhead for you to have had time to shoot it in front. In this case the footwork is the same, but after the first shot you must take the butt off your shoulder, at the same time keeping the *muzzles* on the line of flight of the bird. Your left hand is then up in front of your face, the butt is under your right forearm, and you take the pace round to your rear with the muzzles held constantly in the line between your eye and the target. Having settled your stance with your left foot now pointing in the opposite direction to that in which you were

48 Muzzles on line of target
The demonstrator presents the
gun to you so that you can see it
as if you were holding it yourself:
butt under forearm, muzzles well
up, following the line of the bird
as you turn round to take a shot
behind

49 Left hand on line of target
Here is the gun for a low bird:
butt about level with hip, muzzles
safely up in the air, and you are
following the bird with your
left forefinger, even though the
finger is out of sight behind the
barrels

originally facing, you mount the gun and the muzzles pass *down*
the line of flight of the bird. Keep the swing going, lean forward
on the left foot and fire. The muzzles must be moving down for
this shot, otherwise you will miss behind, which in this case is over
the top. Never try to turn round with the butt at your shoulder;
you are bound to wobble off the line of the bird and you will not
be able to regain your balance before the bird is out of range.

In this last case of the high bird you kept the muzzles on as you
turned, but you will appreciate that with a low bird, or a target
on the ground, keeping the muzzles on would mean that they
would be pointing dangerously low. Therefore you are asked, in
those cases, to hold the line of the target with your left forefinger.
(See Photographs 48 to 52.)

50 Turning for shot behind
A partridge is shot in front,
reasonably high, and another
follows on a similar but lower
course

51 The shooter cannot take
this second bird immediately
because of the Gun on her
right. She continues pivoting
from the hips but lowers her
gun, keeping the muzzles up,
her left hand on the line
between her eye and the
target. She is taking a step
round with her left leg

52 She has moved her left
foot right round so that she
faces to the rear, still keeping
her left hand on the target;
she brings up the butt and as
the muzzles come on she fires,
scoring again. The other Gun
admires the right-and-left

Returning to our ground game, we should realize that rabbit
shooting is different from hare shooting in many ways. The rabbit
is much smaller than the hare and it is also more vulnerable; it is
also usually shot at shorter ranges, often at only about 10 or 15
yards. Rabbit shooting calls for speed and it can be great sport,
remembering always the danger element when there may be dogs
and beaters and even perhaps ferrets in the neighbourhood. When
you are expecting rabbits, stand still and keep quiet; if you are in
a ride through a wood, or watching such a gap from outside the
wood, stand on the side from which the rabbits will be driven.
Have your gun down and pointing loosely towards your side of
the ride, and as soon as you see a rabbit, bend forward from the

hips, for you will certainly be shooting downwards (unless the ride slopes up) swing your gun smartly through the animal, all the time watching its head, and shoot as you pass the head. Do not alter your normal stance or the position of your left hand on the barrels; keep your cheek well on to the stock and do not try to snap at the opposite side of the ride where you hope the rabbit may run into your shot.

In more open conditions rabbit shooting is easier, as long as you remember to bend forward from the hips and to speed up your actions, so that you still adopt the principle of lining up the muzzles between your eye and the target but you waste as little time as possible in order to catch the rabbit before it dodges into cover.

Again, try to watch the animal's head and ears and avoid looking at that white scut which can so easily catch the eye and divert the shot away from the real target.

The sitting shot should be a 100 per cent certain kill but it is often missed. You may want to shoot a sitting rabbit or hare and you may also have an opportunity of taking a sitting pigeon when one flies into a tree near your hide. You may be tempted to 'make sure' of this easy shot, and so you try to sight your shotgun like a rifle; this is most unlikely to produce success. The best way to take a sitter is to watch it carefully for a moment, and then to mount the gun normally but with the thought that you have a bayonet on the end; thrust out your imaginary bayonet as if you were going to skewer the target, and fire as butt and shoulder meet. In this way you will be relying correctly on your first aim and as long as the target is in range you cannot help but cover it with the shot pattern. Remember, however, that a sitting bird is a smaller target than when it is flying; the vulnerable area of a sitting pigeon is probably smaller than your hand, so that you will be well advised to use the left, choked, barrel at ranges of 20 yards or more. It is possible to aim carefully at a sitter but many people have the most inexplicable misses when they do this, and whether they aim at the bird's feet, or blot it out with the muzzles, it flies off unconcernedly and makes the shooter think he must be using blank cartridges. The best method, the shotgun way, the way that will give you confidence in your first aim is to mount the gun normally and use your imaginary bayonet.

The snap shot sometimes appears to be a brilliant one and when witnessed by others it often invokes congratulations for the shooter, who is pleased and most probably considerably surprised as well. In the minds of many shooting men this shot is vaguely defined as aiming at the place the target is going to, and not where it is at the moment. They think of a rabbit crossing a ride or a woodcock flitting through a gap in the trees; they imagine there is no time to swing and so the shooter merely chucks up his gun to the shoulder and fires in front of his target. If he hits it they congratulate him but if he misses they are not surprised. The fact is that the so-called 'snap' shot was really only a quick shot done in the orthodox way, and if it was successful the reason was that there was no time to do it any other way; the shooter put the muzzle of his gun right on the line of the target, followed through and pulled the trigger as he passed it, and that is precisely what this book is trying to teach you to do. The danger lies in the fact that an indifferent performer may bring off what he calls a 'snap' shot and think that he has found a good way of connecting with his target. If he tries out his technique of 'shooting in front', 'aiming where the bird is going to be', on a normal shot when there is plenty of time he will poke at the bird and miss.

If you have success with a so-called 'snap' shot you can profit from the experience by realizing that you performed a well-placed quick shot, and that for other normal shots you can do the same; when you have plenty of time you can use it to line up the target carefully through the muzzles, butt still down, and so be more certain of holding the bird's line correctly, and then mount the gun smoothly and swiftly, feeling certain you have a kill as the trigger is pulled. The poor performer with his 'snap' shot either does not know what he has done, but is agreeably surprised, or he thinks he knows what happened and he is wrong. You, however, will carry out the correct drill, but speeding up a little, and as you gain confidence in your shooting you will become certain of success.

You have now learnt something of the main types of shot and, whether you are a complete beginner or a man of some experience, the chances are that when you try to put this teaching into effect in the field you will miss quite often, and you may become disappointed. As a novice it is easy to learn from scratch, provided you are keen, but the man who has done quite a bit of shooting has also acquired several bad habits and if he tries to follow the teaching in this book he will have to break those habits and learn good ones instead; if you are in this situation you will find that there are times when you shoot partly as taught here and partly in your old, bad way, and as you will inevitably miss the target under those conditions you may feel frustrated and be tempted to forsake the new, the strange, the apparently awkward, even if it is supposed to be correct, and go back to the old familiar, idle methods which at least gave you a few kills sometimes. Resist this wicked thought, and persevere because it will surely be worth while, provided you practise. More of that later, in Chapter 10, but for now we will assume you are trying to do your practice actually in the shooting field and the results are disappointing. What can you do about it?

First of all, do not be over anxious; try to remember that shooting is a sport and that it does not matter if you miss. This is not easy, because you may fear that if you put up a poor performance you will be laughed at and if you are a guest you may not be asked again. But you must try to keep a light-hearted attitude towards shooting and you should regard the other Guns as your friends, not as competitors, and think of the keepers and beaters and loaders and watchers-over-gates as allies, not as enemies looking eagerly for a mistake which they can seize upon and gloat over, to your discomfort. Many misses are caused by anxiety, so if you become fussed and worried when shooting in company try to cultivate a 'What the hell – ?' frame of mind; it has even been claimed that it is no bad thing to work up a certain amount of anger against your next target, after several have been missed, on the lines of, 'I'm jolly well going to swipe this blighter out of the sky!' Then you throw up your gun at it, swing fast and true and score a kill. Such behaviour can cure a bout of poking, but real temper-lost anger will never do because, besides being unseemly, it will allow you to drop back into your worst bad habits.

To shoot well you need confidence and that confidence must extend to believing that what you are trying to do is correct. Convince yourself that misses are virtually always behind and strive to make your swing go through and out in front. It is a natural reaction to want to shoot *at* a bird rather than away in front of it, even though it is moving, and even though the gun is moving as it is fired. That is why it is so easy to stop the swing at the critical moment when it ought to be continued, and why so much emphasis has been given to the fact that misses are usually behind the target. You have been taught to swing and make some forward allowance, especially at longish crossing shots; if you find that you are missing, take a chance, be brave and swing out further in front than you think necessary; when you have a kill, although you felt you were overdoing the lead a bit, you will be confident of swinging out there again. If you miss those long crossers, or the high overhead shots, put a bit of courage into your shooting: try to miss in front. When you connect with the target you will have learnt the lesson that what you were taught was correct, and you will have gained a little more confidence and experience.

One of the difficulties about putting the teaching to practical effect is that thinking about what you should do for a particular shot takes a few seconds, but actually doing it seems to take almost no time, and it is all over and you have missed again before you have been able to start checking the sequence of actions. This stresses the importance of gun handling which should be practised so often that it can be depended upon to be nearly always perfect. In fact, there is always more time for a shot than you think, but it is a common mistake for a beginner to be put off by a sudden flurry of wings, especially when a partridge covey gets up, and merely to shoot off his gun somewhere in the birds' direction without making any preparation for the shot. Two main causes of missing are being too quick and being too slow. Shooting too quickly is caused by being too slow at the start of the shot; if the bird seems to be practically on top of you before you have done anything about it you may become flustered and try to shoot without any preparation and when quite out of control; over-excitement can increase this loss of control and may cause such hasty shooting that both barrels are fired, without result, and you then find yourself still with time enough for one good, controlled shot but only an empty gun in your hands. The remedy for this over-hastiness is to be ready and expectant, and if you are caught somewhat unprepared *make* yourself take the necessary time to get prepared, and then pick your target and shoot calmly and deliberately, perhaps only with one barrel. Do not fire at all if the opportunity is so fleeting that you really have not time to shoot properly, for there is no point in wasting shots.

Shooting too slowly means spending any appreciable time with the gun at the shoulder, and aiming with the barrels, and trying to make sure. This stops the swing and is fatal to your shooting, but not to the target. The rhythm of your shooting must be steady and it consists of picking up the target, swinging through and firing; to help you keep the timing right you may find it helpful to murmur to yourself, as you do the appropriate actions: 'Pick up – swing – shoot.' Unfortunately, it is quite easy to forget to do this, even if you intend to, but when you can remember it you will thereby be prevented from shooting too slowly.

The goal to strive for is to know the reason for every miss, and if you make yourself pause and puzzle it out you very often will be able to fix on at least one fault. Sometimes, however, when birds are plentiful, as at a good pheasant stand or when pigeon are coming in well to the decoys, you may realize after a dozen shots, 'Well, I only hit three of those and I have not the slightest idea whether I kept my cheek on the stock or lifted it too soon.'

It may be that if you have missed a shot and you go through the motions of gun mounting again, immediately afterwards, you will feel that your left leg is bent and not braced, or you can see that your stance is wrong because your feet are too wide apart or the weight is on the right foot. Resolve to correct these for subsequent shots.

You know that there is normally plenty of time at the start of the shot, when you first see the target, so make yourself say, 'Muzzle on' as you prepare for the shot. Then, perhaps, say, 'Lean' as you mount the gun, and so remind yourself to keep your weight forward over the left foot. That will mean that you will have ensured that at least two parts of the drill are correct.

After a few shots you may be struck by that notion of wondering if you kept your cheek well on to the stock. So decide that you *really* are going to next time, that you are going to stand there with the gun up, cheek hugging the stock while you say to yourself, 'Look, I *have* kept my cheek there!' Very likely you will be able to add, 'And, by Golly, I've got that bird, too!' And so will be born a little more of that confidence you need so much.

Perhaps while you are waiting between shots you may think, 'Wonder if I really am putting the muzzles on first and not just throwing the gun up and waving the barrels about? It's the correct way, isn't it?' Select a target in front of you, perhaps the top of a fence post; deliberately hold the gun out in front of you, butt under the forearm, muzzles in the line from your eye to the top of the post; reach forward and mount the gun to your shoulder. Your eye will confirm that the barrels are pointing dead on target: more confidence ensues and you look forward eagerly to the next shot when you are going to put the teaching into effect. This example could not, of course, be safely carried out at a pheasant stand but it could very well be done in a pigeon hide.

Before you start shooting for the day make several practice swings. You may have plenty of time if you are waiting for pigeon or duck. Swing on to rooks or plover, starlings and waders and any other birds that you are not intending to shoot. If you are in company waiting for pheasants or partridges do not be shy about loosening up with some practice swings; do not be put off by imagining that the other Guns will think you are showing off; they will not think so if they have any manners and if they are as keen about shooting well as you are.

It is a good rule during a shoot never to look at any bird which is likely to come in range, *except over the muzzles*. Thus, a bird flies over your neighbour but towards you: 'If he misses, I'll have

53 Retrieving The most accurate shot still needs help from a dog to collect his birds, particularly when they fall in thick cover. Here a labrador brings in a grouse

a go,' you think as you watch, with your gun pointing down to the ground in a normal waiting position. He does miss, and suddenly there is the bird practically on top of you, flying fast; you whip up the gun, take a hurried shot, and miss too. Had you been watching that bird over your muzzles, it would have been quite simple to lower the gun again if your neighbour's shot had been successful. *But* you would have been instantly ready to take advantage of his miss, raise the butt, swing on and kill the bird. Many misses are caused through failing to carry out this preparation drill, as when a bird flies down the line of Guns and is saluted all the way; each Gun just casually watches his neighbour, but doesn't realize that the bird is now *his* until it is too late to mount the gun correctly. (See photograph 58.)

54 A shot taken behind The shooter's front is away from the camera, as indicated by the shooting stick to his rear and the number peg in front. He is here facing his right and is taking a line on a highish pheasant, crossing from front to rear

55 A shot taken behind He has swung round to take the bird very
nearly behind him and without moving his feet. The weight is still on his
left foot and his body has pivoted round so that his chest is still oblique to
the target. This is good style, the result of practice and training the body to
perform the required movements. Out-of-training shooters find this position
awkward and uncomfortable; the ability to adopt it easily is useful in saving
the time needed to step round for the shot, and it avoids changing a good
foot platform for a doubtful one, as on rough ground or on a steep slope;
it is valuable to the wildfowler whose feet are stuck in the mud

Be relaxed while you are waiting for birds to appear but at the same time keep alert. As you gain more experience in the field you should learn the habits of the birds you shoot so that, for example, you are able to say where a covey will probably be when walking-up partridges. Listen for the alarm calls of jays and cock pheasants, always watch the behaviour of dogs when they are hunting or retrieving. Learn to identify birds at long distances by the pattern and rate of their wing beats. As your knowledge of all these subjects improves you will be able to anticipate the appearance of your quarry and you will be more likely to deal with it effectively than if you are caught unawares. In order to learn these things you need to be curious and to seek help from other more experienced countrymen. Occasionally you will find shooting men who know very little about the game they shoot, and are apparently not sufficiently interested to try to find out more; they miss a great deal of the joy of shooting which can only be found after a study of natural history and game rearing, vermin destruction, planning drives, methods of beating, the training and use of dogs, and after acquiring a reasonable knowledge of ballistics and the functioning of guns. Most shooting men, however, are interested in these matters and they will be glad to help and advise you if you ask about them. Never fail to take an opportunity for a chat with a gamekeeper; he will always be happy that someone is taking an interest in his work, and the amount of concentrated sound sense and practical knowledge that most good 'keepers can command is sometimes surprising and always quite fascinating.

The more you learn about everything that occurs in the shooting field the more chance you have of being a good shot, and of increasing your enjoyment therefrom.

If you follow the instruction in this book you can teach yourself to shoot, up to a point. You must then acquire experience and after that you should consult an expert to spot your faults and advise you about correcting them. Then you can go back to getting some more experience, and so the cycle continues. If you are a beginner, and you can afford the time and expense, you ought to consult the expert before you start looking for much experience, in order to acquire a few good habits before you learn too many bad ones. But even if you can make a few visits to a shooting school you will still drop into some bad habits when you are actually out shooting, so catechize yourself occasionally, run through in your mind the various points in the drill and put them right one by one.

Persevere in your struggle to find a good style. Each miss is caused by a fault in style and when the style is right the result of the shot is a foregone conclusion, without any need to look at the target for confirmation.

The best way to put shooting instruction into effect is to keep in practice; your body should be trained to perform the required movements without conscious thought and effort. We shall have more to say on practice in Chapter 10. (Photographs 54 and 55 illustrate good body control.)

8 Specific targets

When discussing certain shots, such as the horizontal crosser or the going-away bird, various principles have been established about the correct method of dealing with the situation. But a specific target, by which is meant a certain species of bird, may require some extra considerations because of its habits, its flying characteristics and the circumstances of its shooting. These we shall consider in this chapter.

Pheasants are usually associated in the shooting man's mind with 'high birds', although in fact the majority of the birds in the bag at the end of a normal shooting day will probably have been shot at a range of only about 20 to 25 yards; 100 feet up in the air looks remarkably high, and it is more than twice the height of the trees in an average pheasant covert. 40 yards up looks so high that inexperienced Guns are apt to reckon that a pheasant at that height is out of range; it is not out of range of the gun but it may be beyond the range of the skill of the shooter. These high birds are usually produced by pushing them out of a wood on the side of a hill so that they fly across the valley at the bottom of which the Guns are standing. The result is that they can often be seen approaching for some time before they come into range.

When there is plenty of time to watch a bird there may be a tendency to put the gun up too soon, and then have to hang in an aiming position waiting for the bird to come into range. This obviously means a slow swing or virtually no swing at all, and the shot is almost certain to miss even if some forward allowance has

56 **A difficult stance**   A miss at a pheasant which has swung round over the valley behind the Gun, whose front was originally towards the left side of the picture. A difficult shot on the side of the hill, but not made any easier by the rather wide stance; in this case, however, a step round with the left foot would probably have been difficult because of the rough ground

been given. To prevent this state of affairs the advice is sometime given that the shooter who sees his bird high and far away should note its probable course and then look down for a second or two; when he looks up again the bird will be in range, somewhere just overhead, and he can swing up quickly and shoot it. This theory is correct in as much as the shot will have to be taken quickly and therefore a slow poke is hardly possible, but the shot will very likely be erratic and out of control and it is not the way to shoot pheasants. It is, in fact, throwing away the precious advantage on your side when shooting driven pheasants, which is that most of them fly determinedly to some cover behind you in the manner worked out by your host when he planned the drive. If you are shooting duck or pigeon you will be advised to keep your head down when you see an out-of-range bird approaching because otherwise it will sheer away when it sees you; but not so with pheasants.

For the high approaching pheasant you should prepare for the shot in the normal way and never take your eyes off the bird. As it comes into range just take the shot with the same timing as you would if you had not had a few extra seconds to wait before the gun was mounted. Your timing is most important and it is individual to you and you should try not to alter it; nor should you try to copy someone else's. Remember, when deciding whether the bird is in range, that you are going to shoot it in front of you and not directly overhead. Your swing will carry on to a point above you, or even slightly further, but your brain must give the order to fire while the bird is still well in front.

There is another technique for shooting these high overhead birds which helps to avoid the difficulty caused by losing sight of them at the moment of firing, especially if the shooter likes to dim his left eye, and so lose binocular vision. This is to twist the upper body sideways so that the shoulders, instead of being at right angles to the bird's line of flight, are parallel to it. The shot then becomes, in effect, a horizontal crosser and no longer a vertical one. Some people find it easier to form their 'picture' in this way, and to swing ahead to give the necessary lead to this high bird which they can still see.

---

57 **A pheasant over the valley**   Another shot at a pheasant crossing slightly behind the Gun. As the ground is firm stubble the left foot could well have been moved round across the slope. Good footwork helps good style

Although pheasants generally fly straight, in as much as they go for a specific objective and are little deterred by the sight of humans or the sound of gunfire, they do sometimes curl round so that they fly on a curved path, and they do this particularly when they are high and when there is a cross wind. The curl is of the bird's own determination but even if it is intending to fly straight a strong wind will cause it to drift sideways. The shooter, therefore, needs to watch for both curl and drift, and perhaps both at once.

If you are shooting a high overhead pheasant with a wind blowing to one side of it, the bird's drift to leeward will usually be more than you realize, especially as it is difficult to appreciate the drift against a background of sky. You should therefore note the wind direction and, instead of bringing the gun up through the bird's tail and head, you should swing through the tip of its downwind wing and still give it the same forward allowance as you would have done without a wind to worry about. Note that there will be a tendency when swinging through the bird's wing to give less lead than normal and this must not happen. A curling overhead bird that is also drifting across the wind may need even more sideways allowance, the gun being swung through beyond the tip of its leeward wing. If you see a pheasant in front of you, but not very high, and it is curling to one side instead of coming straight at you the effect of the curling movement will be less if you delay the shot for a second or so until the bird has become practically a crosser, when the curling will be away from you and not across as well. The curler must be watched carefully and the shot taken, as far as you are able, when the effect of the curl least from your position.

The gliding pheasant presents another set of problems, especially as it may be curling as well. The first point to understand is that a pheasant is nearly always going faster when it is gliding than when it is flapping its wings, whereas at first sight one might well assume that it must be going slower. The reason for the gliding speed is that the bird is descending and it is going too fast to be able to propel itself by flapping and so it glides on set wings. The analogy is a man pedalling a bicycle downhill: as his speed increases he cannot pedal with effect any more and so he free-wheels. Your free-wheeling pheasant may be going very fast indeed, so give it plenty of forward allowance and remember that the dropping effect of the glide will require the gun to be swung down the bird's line, down under its throat and not out over the back of its head as in the case of a rising bird.

Now for partridges, shot when walking-up or as driven birds: their characteristic, so often forgotten or ignored, is that they have very good hearing and they are remarkably quick to take evasive action as soon as they are aware of something suspicious. So quick and clever are they that if the Guns talk and shout, while planning a walking-up manoeuvre or waiting for birds to be driven, the chances are that most of the partridges in the neighbourhood will run off elsewhere without even being seen.

Assuming that you have been careful and quiet enough to approach a covey when walking-up, your first difficulty is to persuade yourself that there is time for deliberate shooting when the birds suddenly spring into the air. If you try to hurry you will not even have your stance correct, especially if you are on uneven ground, going through roots or over plough. Therefore you must first stop walking, with the left foot in front and, keeping your eye on the bird you have chosen, and even though you think the bird is going away in a tremendous hurry and will be out of range in about half a second, place your muzzles on and mount the gun as you have been taught. Stick to your timing; one deliberate shot is better than two blazed off into the air. With experience your timing will speed up until it approaches that of the expert who can pick two birds out of a covey before the poor shot has put his gun to his shoulder. The small partridge with its quick wing beats appears to be very fast, but it is slower than the pheasant. Remember on this going-away shot to note the position of the bird's head and so decide whether it is rising or moving to the right or the left; if it is going to one side swing your gun through its wing on that side to help keep the shot inside the bird's course.

When walking-up you should note carefully where your birds drop, and also watch those of other Guns when they are shooting and you are not. When you reach the fall, if you do not see the bird immediately, drop your hat or handkerchief on the ground to mark the spot as you begin searching around.

If you are shooting driven partridges you should keep quiet as you go to your stand and while you are waiting. The beaters may be a mile away but it is possible for a covey to be just over the hedge within 50 yards of you. Try and relax while you are waiting and do not strain your eyes, peering anxiously in all directions. Generally a whistle is blown by the 'keeper when the beaters put up a covey; when you hear this look above the hedge in front of you at nothing in particular, and when the covey appears seize on to the first bird that catches your eye and shoot it. The exploding

covey coming over a hedge is even more unnerving than the one which jumps out of a field when you are walking-up, and in each case the success of the shot depends on immediately deciding which bird you are going to shoot, and sticking to it even though you see another bird out of the corner of your eye which seems to be a bit closer and therefore, temptingly, easier. If you are standing behind a high hedge and you cannot see the covey until it scatters over your head you may have to turn and take the shot behind; that is all right, but remember to keep your eye on one bird as you turn, and to keep the gun muzzles up out of danger.

If you can see well out in front you will have a better chance of scoring with both barrels if you first choose a bird some way back in the covey, shoot it in front at about 35 yards, and then carry through the swing on to one of the leading birds, as described in Chapter 6. But if there is plenty of time to choose any bird you wish, it would be better, especially early in the season, to shoot the leading bird of the covey first, because the old birds normally lead and if they are shot the covey breaks up and is more likely to appear in small numbers over the Guns on future occasions, instead of the whole lot going over one Gun.

Partridges normally fly low but they are sometimes driven over belts of trees to provide higher shots. Their flying characteristic then is to come down low again fairly quickly and not to glide, as pheasants do.

The successful partridge shooter needs a phlegmatic temperament which will not allow him to get flustered by the sudden appearance of the birds, nor cause him to want to chatter to his neighbours while he is waiting. Remember always to pick a bird in the covey; do not fire 'into the brown' or you will hit what you aim at, which is the space between the partridges. When you have to choose a bird quickly, it is the one which first catches your eye.

Grouse may be walked-up or driven and the shots when walking-up produce no problems very different to those met with partridges. You may get very close to a squatting grouse, especially when using pointers or setters, and if this happens take plenty of time and let the bird get 20 yards or so away before you shoot it.

---

58 The wrong way to look at a bird   Bad form. He is watching a bird approaching his neighbour. but he is *not* looking at it over the ends of his barrels. See page 111

Driven grouse provide a form of shooting especially their own, and it needs studying. When you arrive at the butts you should look at them with safety in mind, because when they are sited across the slope of a hill a high butt may be in a dangerous position if the occupant of the next-door lower butt is inclined to swing his gun across the line. Also, the line itself is often not straight, but slightly curved so that a flank Gun may be ahead of those in the centre. Swinging down the line should never happen, of course, but dangerous shots are sometimes taken at grouse in the excitement of the moment, and butts often have a post each side designed to prevent a gun being swung too far towards the neighbouring butt (Photograph 62). The post, however, can be somewhat upsetting to the shooter if it is so placed that he sees it and begins to slow down his swing while he is still well within the zone in which he can shoot safely; consequently the experienced shot is apt to shoot from the front edge of the butt, or perhaps take down the marker sticks, and he relies on forming a V in his mind's eye inside which it is safe to shoot, and if a bird crosses outside the arms of the V he leaves it to the neighbouring Gun. Whatever safety marks are put out at your butt, and it is always possible that there may not be any, have a good look round and decide where you can shoot safely and also where birds might appear which could seem to be shootable but which must be left to the next Gun. Dangerous shots are unintentional, but they are caused by lack of thought for others, and over-excitement. Self discipline is necessary and a careful study of the situation before shooting begins.

When you have settled in your butt, watch your front but do not tire your eyes searching for birds long before they are likely to appear; at the same time you should realize that grouse tend to keep low, following the contours of the ground and they can be difficult to spot against the heather. When the birds are coming do not hide behind the front parapet of the butt and then bob up to take a shot, but stand up and keep still so that the covey comes on and does not scatter, while it is out of range, on seeing a sudden movement. Try to take your first bird as far out as you reasonably

59 **A Rising pheasant** A good position for a shot at a pheasant over the trees; the gun is still swinging well, but the first barrel has missed, probably low; the attitude of the bird indicates that it is rising, and emphasizes the need for trying to shoot above its neck, as described in Chapter 6

can; if you pick it up at about 60 yards it will be only 40 yards out by the time you shoot, and that is a reasonable distance for a grouse coming straight at you. If you wait too long you will smash the bird at too short a range and you will have no time for a second shot in front. It is better, when you first meet driven grouse, to concentrate on having one good shot in front, and not to try to fire off both barrels in a hurry. Particularly if you are unused to the open country of grouse moors it will be worth your while to pace out 40 yards in front of the butt and note some feature such as a rock that you can see when you are back in the butt; you can then try to pick up the birds when they are further away than your ranging mark, although when actually shooting it is scarcely possible to see either ranging or safety marks because all your attention is fixed on the target.

Because the birds tend to keep low, hanging in the aim is especially reprehensible; remember to shoot on first aim and when you turn to take a shot behind, drop the butt off the shoulder, keep the gun muzzles up but follow the flight of the bird with your left forefinger, as described on pages 102–103. The open nature of the country means that the effect of a wind on the birds is greater than in more enclosed conditions; you will naturally swing fast on birds coming downwind but you will need to remind yourself to swing through birds which are flying upwind; sometimes they appear almost to hang in the wind and you will be tempted to shoot *at* them, because they look so easy. The slow bird is generally more difficult than the fast one because it needs more conscious effort to shoot away in front of it instead of directly at it.

Shooting with a pair of guns is described on pages 142–6. The loader in a grouse butt needs to be especially efficient if he is to be an asset and not a hindrance, particularly because when things happen they happen fast and the butt itself limits the space available for movement. The loader must keep still while birds are approaching. Even if you do not use two guns a loader to carry the cartridges is a great help; grouse shooting involves plenty of exercise over difficult ground and no one can shoot well if he is physically exhausted.

Snipe provide wonderful sport but they can also cause a longer

---

60 **Grouse approaching**   When grouse shooting you must learn to pick one bird only out of the covey to shoot at. Note well-built butt of stone, topped with turf

61 High Grouse
Sometimes grouse fly quite high, offering overhead shots not unlike pheasant shooting

62 Low grouse
Grouse more frequently fly low. Here one has been shot and the Gun raises his muzzles to turn and take another bird after it has passed the butt. Note safety sticks on butt to deter shooting down the line

run of misses than almost any bird. They rise unexpectedly and fly in twists and turns and the marshland they frequent does not make it any easier for the shooter to find a firm stance. Advice is sometimes given to snipe shooters to fire at once, as soon as the bird jumps into the air and before it has had time to start jinking, but this is nearly always impossible. In any case, the first and most essential piece of advice is that the shooter should *not* be in a frantic hurry. Has it occurred to you that the zigzag flight of a snipe going away from you gives you more time to shoot than if it was travelling straight, like a partridge?

You cannot mount your gun for a snipe and then follow its flight, as you will find that the gun is going one way while the bird is going another. The correct drill is to hold the muzzle on the bird directly you see it, and keep the muzzle on, butt down below your forearm, while the bird flicks to the left, then swing the muzzle across as it goes to the right, then again left and you can then probably decide to take the shot as the bird goes right again; when the right handed jink starts you mount the gun and fire. You can shoot on the earliest jink that makes you feel confident you are going to be on the target, and that will usually be the third or fourth. Once you have mastered the technique of always putting the *muzzle* on all your birds, and getting the line before you bring up the *butt*, you will find this method of snipe shooting can turn what is always reckoned to be a tricky shot into a comparatively easy one.

Even if a snipe gets up a fair way ahead, say 20 yards, there is still time to go through the sequence described above because the deviations to right and left cause the bird to remain in range for a comparatively long time. Resist the desire to fire off a shot desperately quickly, and instead take a steady, calculated one after following the bird's erratic flight with the muzzle. You must be alert and not waste time planting your feet firmly in the correct position as soon as a bird appears, and if you miss a shot you should watch the bird because it may well land not very far away, and give you a chance to approach it again. Use no. 8 shot, for preference.

Driven snipe look extraordinarily small to the shooter who is used to seeing pheasants over his head, but they do not fly high and you can reckon they are always in range if they pass more or less over you. They still fly from side to side but they do not create the same urgent panic in the shooter to fire in a hurry, because

63 An under-and-over gun   A grouse dead in the air. An under-and-over gun is being used, often a favourite with Contintental sportsmen

they are coming towards him. The drill of picking them up with the muzzle is the same; if you follow them thus for two or three runs you should then be able to choose the next one when you feel you can mount the gun and know it is going with the bird and not in the opposite direction.

Woodcock are not easy to hit but the erratic and dangerous shooting that so often follows the warning cry of 'Woodcock forward'! is not really excusable. There is often an extra keenness among the Guns to be credited with a 'cock, perhaps because they want to eat it, for the man who shoots a woodcock is usually given it at the end of the day, or perhaps because they want another pin feather to put in their hats, or possibly even from a mildly immodest desire to be considered a good shot; whatever the cause of this excitability, the fact is that woodcock do bring an element of danger into what was previously a reasonable staid pheasant shoot. In certain parts of Great Britain, particularly East Anglia and the West Country, special woodcock shoots are held at the end of the year but over the rest of the country only occasional birds are met when they migrate from Europe during November.

The chief characteristics of the woodcock that affect shooting men are that when driven out of cover it seeks the shadows and consequently in a wood it dodges between trees and round bushes, and never flies very high. In the open it flies straight and it is not very fast, certainly slower than a pheasant. If you put up a woodcock in a wood you should follow it with the gun muzzles as it dodges through the trees and try to take it in an opening between the trees; this is a difficult shot and if there are other people about and the bird keeps low you ought not to shoot but merely cry, 'Woodcock!' and hope someone else may have a safer shot in the open. If you are in the open and the shout of, ' 'Cock Forr'ard!' is heard, try to check the surge of excitement you will feel and watch carefully for the bird to appear; when it does, watch it as others fire because you may see a gun pointing your direction and so find it prudent to fall flat on your face. But assuming the shooting is safe, keep your eye on the bird because, although it will not dodge about as it does among trees, it will change direction occasionally and it may come towards you. If it does, treat it as a perfectly normal shot, watch its line past the end of your barrels and swing through and shoot.

Wildfowling is a special branch of shooting outside the scope of this book but a certain amount of instruction follows about the actual shooting of duck and geese. Duck can hear and see well and they use these senses to keep away from trouble; they also fly high and when shot at will always climb still higher, so never shoot at them at maximum range and especially if they are circling with the obvious intention of coming down lower. When you fire at a flight of duck always be ready to swing up higher for a second barrel because they will certainly rise even if they have not seen you.

Two difficulties experienced when wildfowling, not inland duck shooting at flight ponds, are concerned with footwork in the mud and swinging a gun when encumbered with extra clothing.

Warm clothing is necessary because you cannot shoot straight if you are too cold, but the bulk of the clothing can be reduced a little by wearing thin layers near the skin rather than thick jerseys and jackets on top. However, the wildfowler cannot expect the gun which was fitted to him in normal clothes to be equally comfortable when he is in his 'fowling kit: the stock will be too long. If a special wildfowling gun is used it ought to be fitted with the owner wearing his thick clothes, but if you use your normal game gun for your coastal forays you can overcome the apparently long stock by pushing your arms and gun as far out in front as possible just before you take a shot; the movement is similar to 'shooting a cuff' and it will remove some of the folds of thick clothing from your shoulders, and assist gun mounting. If you avoid having a top jacket made of any material which gets sticky when wet, and also have a plain wooden butt with no rubber recoil pad, you will help the butt to slide easily into the shoulder. If you find your clothing very much in the way so that the butt really is being pushed forward more than usual you can hold the gun with the left hand a little further down the barrels than normal; but this shortened grip is no excuse for bending the left arm unduly and its attitude should remain the same as for shooting in ordinary clothes.

A basic rule for footwork in the mud is to accept the fact that it is best not to try to do any. But remember that it is possible, with the feet firmly fixed in the ground, to swing from the hips for considerably more than a right angle to each side. When you have to crouch down in a ditch or behind some reeds while the birds approach it is always better to stand up to take the shot, if you

---

64 The exploding covey   A covey of partridges bursts over the hedge. Which bird have you selected?

can. If you cannot stand and must shoot from a sitting or kneeling position, it is particularly important to have a few practice swings in your cramped position before the duck appear. It is possible to swing the body quite a long way round when sitting down, and a little practice at home sitting on a chair or kneeling on the floor and holding a gun will show you what can be done; what you have to make yourself do, encumbered in heavy clothes and squatting on the slippery, muddy bank of a gutter, is to twist the upper part of your body round to face the target and not try to shoot with the body stiff and the arms swinging across it. Keep your head in a natural upright position and be careful that the drag of the heavy clothing across your shoulders does not make you drop your face to the stock, instead of bringing the stock up to the cheek as you should do. You must make every effort to obtain the maximum movement for your swing, because so many things are tending to constrict it: cold, stiffness, long waits with no shooting, and the almost inevitable anxiety to connect when you do have a shot.

Estimating range is particularly important on the foreshore, when you can expect to shoot birds of varying species, and the apparent size of a duck may not necessarily indicate its range; for instance, a lowish teal looks the same size as a high mallard and to shoot wildfowl properly you must learn to distinguish different species at a glance, by their silhouette, or their wing beats or their call. If you do not know your birds you ought not to shoot; only experience can teach you and the man who is not prepared to learn is not keen enough to go wildfowling; he should give it up.

Shooting 'fowl at dawn and dusk often means shooting in the dark. It is practically always better to stand up for this as the birds will not see you if you keep still. This is where good gun mounting counts for so much because you must listen for the duck, and when you hear the call or the wing beats you have only time for a quick look up, and as you see a dark shape against the sky your gun must come up and point where your eye is looking, immediately. This is the one exception to the rule of putting the muzzles on the target before mounting the gun; in this case you cannot see the line of the bird before it appears overhead and for this reason only you are permitted to shoot as quickly as possible, relying on

65 **One killed and one to come** One dead in the air and the shooter swinging well on to the second. Note that the gun is pointing ahead of the pheasant

the gun following your eye. Remember to push your arms out quickly to free your shoulders from your heavy clothing. Some 'fowlers like to have a special foresight on their guns which they say helps them to see the barrels in the dark; some put a blob of mud on the end of the barrels or a piece of chewing gum. Enlarging the foresight indicates wrong thinking because you should not want to see the barrels; all your concentration should be on the difficult task of seeing the duck, and a correctly mounted gun will point where you look.

Geese present no very different problem from duck in their actual shooting except that their large size increases the likelihood of them being shot at when out of range. Remember to watch their heads and to swing out well ahead because the slow wing beat gives a false impression that their speed is less than it really is. Use a large size of shot, probably BB or No. 1, and never risk pricking a goose by shooting at it with small shot such as No. 6.

Pigeon can see exceptionally well, especially movement, and they can change direction in flight very quickly. This is not the place to discuss the fascinating business of finding flight lines, setting out decoys and building hides but we will examine some details of how to shoot the birds, over decoys and when coming in to roost.

Your pigeon hide should be about chest height so that you can sit in it while you are waiting for the birds, and can stand up and swing the gun freely. An oil drum is very suitable for sitting on and is much firmer than a shooting stick if you want to take a shot while sitting. The experts often do shoot sitting and they can also frequently shoot a pigeon before it is aware of them. This is difficult and it calls for very quick shooting; you may find that as you bring up your gun the bird sees you, and at the precise moment that you fire it jinks sideways and you know you have missed. If you see the jink in time, and can stop the shot, you should drop the butt off your cheek and a few inches down from your shoulder, push the muzzles over through the pigeon and bring up the gun again to shoot. Do not stay in the aim and chase the bird across with the butt still in your shoulder.

Under certain conditions it is easier to shoot pigeon without them seeing you first; thus, in a strong wind they keep low, only a few feet off the ground, and you can then more easily watch them through the hide and swing the gun quickly over the top when they come into range, than when they fly higher and see you in the hide

almost before they are shootable. Also, if you have a low sun behind you the pigeon will not see you so easily as they come in to
the decoys. But when you cannot get your gun on to the birds without them seeing you and quickly changing direction just as you are
about to fire, the best thing to do is to stand up and let a bird see
you, watch it jink to one side, and then put the muzzles on its new
course and shoot.

There may be occasions when you have only a roughly im-
provised hide, not very tall, and nothing to sit on and so you have
to kneel behind it. It will always be better if you can stand up to
shoot but you may find that as you get to your feet the birds sheer
off out of range before you can fire, and so you decide to shoot
kneeling. This is not easy and you will probably find that there is
a tendency to cant the barrels when you swing out to the side,
and to squat back on to the foot of the leg you are kneeling on
when you take an overhead shot; you must try hard to pivot your
body to either side, just as you would if you were standing, and for
the overhead shot you should sway forward and bend back your
body in the same way that you lean forward when standing. It is
possible to swing up well and keep the swing going if you sway
forward, but once you allow your behind to drop back on to your
rearward foot the swing inevitably comes to a halt before it
reaches the vertical. This point is worth testing at home, kneeling
on the floor, and when you have found the feel of it you will be
able to avoid being in the exasperating position of missing nearly
every pigeon you shoot at while you are kneeling, and hardly ever
getting a decent shot in range when you stand up.

Shooting pigeon as they come in to roost in a wood can be good
sport. A hide is not necessary and the shooter should stand with
his back to a tree and concentrate on the sky in front and above
him and not try to look round in all directions. Ignore the trees
when you see a pigeon coming; pick up the bird with the
muzzles and shoot it in the ordinary way as if there were no trees
there at all. Some of the shot will occasionally hit a branch but
you will be surprised how much gets through. Once you have
mastered the idea of paying no attention to the trees you ought to
kill many birds, because it is fairly easy shooting as they will not
be very high and usually they cannot see you in time to jink out
of the way. When you first attempt this sort of shooting you may
be inclined to think that you must wait for the birds to cross the
gaps between the tree tops but this is not so, because if you do you

will not have many chances and you will probably miss most shots through poking at the gaps and actually firing just after the birds have crossed them.

Pigeon are sometimes spoken of as being difficult to kill because they are tough and can resist shot. This is not so, but the idea arises because a pigeon's feathers are loose and one pellet passing harmlessly across its body will knock out a big bunch of feathers, which gives the inexperienced shooter a false impression that the bird has been squarely hit and is still flying on, thus demonstrating its resistance to shot. They are often difficult to shoot because of their aerobatic skill, but if you hit them properly they will come down, even at 40 yards with No. 6 shot.

No shooting man should ever miss an opportunity to kill vermin and the most likely birds to come his way are crows, magpies and jays. The crow flies with slow wing beats which can tempt you to shoot *at* it instead of swinging through; remember the teaching about shooting birds flying slowly against a wind, and make yourself swing out beyond a crow's beak before you fire. Each one you kill will earn you the gratitude of the owner and 'keeper of the land.

Magpies often have an undulating flight which makes them not easy to shoot. When you see one flying in this way follow it with the gun muzzles, as you did the twists and turns of the snipe, and try to shoot it as it comes up to the top of one of its undulations. Do not hold the gun at your shoulder and try to wave the barrels up and down in time with the magpie.

Jays are easy to shoot if you can get near them, but they are most observant and clever at keeping away from trouble when they see it approaching. Learn to recognize the alarm call of a jay so that when you hear it as the beaters approach you can be on the look-out for the bird to appear out of the wood. Like magpies, they are great egg stealers and they do more harm than good.

Whatever your target, take the shot with confidence and when you miss try to puzzle out at least one probable cause. When you are going out to shoot a particular species of bird for the first time make every effort to find out something about it beforehand, from books and from your friends. Be particularly careful about birds which are protected: study Appendix A.

---

66 Partridges Partridges come suddenly into view. They are often low and so seem faster than they really are. A cool head is needed to pick only one out of so many

9 Loading, safety and shooting rules

Loading is closely associated with cartridge carrying, which was discussed on pages 38–39. Whatever method you adopt for carrying you should also discover which way is most convenient for loading, more particularly when this has to be done at speed.

Many people find it easy to take cartridges from the side pockets of their jackets and it is worth while experimenting to see whether you prefer to use the right or the left pocket. If you think a cartridge belt allows you to grab hold of a round more quickly you may like to try a belt with metal clips to hold the cartridges; these belts are not the best for carrying ammunition, as explained in Chapter 2, but they do allow a cartridge to be pulled quickly out sideways, whereas with a looped belt the cartridge has to be pulled up and out; spring clips become loose with wear and must then be replaced. Belts have the advantages that they hold the cartridges base upwards and they do not add any weight to the wearer's shoulders; all the same, loading from the pocket with a cartridge bag handy on the ground for replenishment is probably the most popular method when quick shooting is expected against driven game. Incidentally, you should practise loading two cartridges at once when both barrels have been fired, and not slow down the operation by putting in one at a time; and practice is necessary if you are to avoid fumbling around in your pocket while you try to take hold of two cartridges with their bases both facing the same way.

A loader can be a great assistance when the birds are coming over well, even when only one gun is used. Indeed, it is unwise to

---

67 A good position A good stance and reach, cheek well bedded onto the stock. The left forefinger would be better if it was pointing straight along the barrels. The loader's gun should be swung round so that its triggers are facing his front, and the barrels resting on his right shoulder

attempt to use two guns until you are a good performer with one. If you have a loader for your one gun you can merely open it after firing, and he will insert fresh cartridges while you keep your eyes on the birds, and you will thus be able to pick up your next target more quickly. Naturally all loading is speeded up if the gun automatically ejects the spent cartridges and the small extra cost of an ejector gun, see page 16, is well worth while, in fact practically essential, if you hope to shoot driven game.

Shooting two guns with a loader requires practice and a recognized drill; the farm worker or gardener who is brought in to load cannot be any help until he has had practice and understands the rules. A loader normally loads from the cartridge bag and it is a good plan for him to give the bag a shake on reaching the stand, because this brings the bases of the cartridges uppermost which makes them easier to pick up in pairs. Some loaders have clips for half a dozen rounds on the outside of their bags for quick use, and some hold two or more cartridges between the fingers of their right hands, ready to put straight into the empty gun without having to dip into the bag; this requires a certain skill and should be done in the field only after practice at home. If you are going to train a loader snap caps are useful so that the guns may be 'fired' and the caps ejected. See Photographs 68 and 69 for pictures of loaders.

All loading and unloading, whether done by yourself or by a loader should be done with the gun barrels pointing downward, and the gun should be closed by raising the stock so that the barrels still point down, and not by bringing the barrels up to the stock. Guns have been known to go off as they were closed, perhaps because a finger strayed on to a trigger or perhaps because the lock was old and worn.

When you have a loader he should stand to your right rear and you should hand him the gun past your right shoulder; even if you swing over to the extreme left to take a shot, do not carry on round to the left but return to face your normal front and hand the gun

68 **Working with a loader**   Each is passing a gun with his right hand and receiving one in his left. The shooter is watching his front and selecting his next target. The loader is watching what he is doing and not gazing at birds in the sky. Safety catches are on, and fingers are off triggers; it would be better it the loader held his gun by the small of the butt, as in Photograph 19. The dog is not well placed and would be less likely to be tripped over if it sat in front of the shooter

69 A well-equipped loader   This loader has eight cartridges carried in clips on the side of his bag, where they can be grabbed quickly and the clips subsequently recharged from the bag. He also holds four rounds between the fingers of his right hand

back to your right. The drill of loading should be as follows:

1 Having fired either one or both barrels the shooter puts on the safety catch and brings the gun back, muzzles up, and held in his right hand so that the breech is about level with his right shoulder.

2 The shooter holds his left hand out beyond the gun, palm open

and facing his rear. Meanwhile he continues to watch his front, looking for his next target.

3 The loader takes hold of the empty, or partially empty gun a few inches above the breech and at the same time places the loaded gun in the shooter's left hand.

4 The shooter grasps the fresh gun around the fore-end and prepares for his next shot.

5 The loader turns slightly to his right, lowers his gun so that the stock comes under his right arm and he can flick it open with his thumb against the top lever and fingers pressing the side of the lock.

6 The loader grasps the gun barrels and pushes them down to eject the cartridges, while his right hand takes the fresh cartridges from his bag.

7 Dropping the cartridges into the breech, the loader raises the stock with his right fingers a few inches behind the trigger guard and then lifts the gun up vertically, holding it with his right hand at the grip, or small of the butt.

8 The loader then turns his body slightly left and is ready to put the loaded gun into the shooter's left hand, and to take the fired gun at the same time.

Note particularly that the guns are always passed across with the safety catch on; to do otherwise does not save time and is dangerous, particularly if the shooter hands back his gun with one unfired cartridge in it. The loader should not turn to his left with the empty gun, and then load it and swing it back to the right with the barrels pointing down at the back of the shooter's legs. This happens more often than anyone realizes, except an observant picker-up standing behind. Do not let your loader think he is helping you by pushing forward the safety catch before he hands you a gun.

While waiting for the birds to appear the shooter must keep his gun barrels down, pointing a yard or two in front of him, or, if he is sitting, a convenient and safe place for the gun is on his right leg, behind the knee, and gripped with the right hand at the small of the butt. He should not lay the gun across his lap so that the barrels point towards his neighbour. The loader should keep his gun barrels pointing up in the air, and a restful way is to hold it in the right hand and rest the barrels on his right shoulder, trigger guards uppermost.

The speed and efficiency of a well-trained pair, loader and Gun, is remarkable to behold but do not think that the shooter is firing so rapidly that he is not bothering to put his muzzles on his targets before he fires; if he is a good shot and is killing his birds you may be sure that the muzzles will be on a split second after his left hand takes a loaded gun, and as the hand goes out to mount the weapon.

Handguards may be fitted to gun barrels to protect the fingers from hot barrels when shooting fast. They must fit tightly because a loose guard could allow the gun to slip through as the shooter takes it and it would fall to the ground, which could be most dangerous. A handguard is normally steel encased in leather and it slides on to the barrels; it can be fixed in position if a special stud is fitted to the gun but usually it is expected to stay in position because of the grip of the spring steel. If the guard slips back it can sometimes depress the fore-end release button and so cause the fore-end to fall off. As well as protecting the hand from heat the guard is comfortable to hold in cold weather even when not shooting fast; it can also be a guide for positioning the left hand but only when firmly fixed, because if it slips back on recoil it can just as easily guide the left hand to the wrong place, too far back by the fore-end; the effect of this will depend on the length of the shooter's arm and the normal position for his left hand grip. Many shooters are content to do without hand-guards and to wear a glove on the left hand instead.

A good loader can render more assistance than merely loading and ammunition carrying, and, of course, having such useful things in his pocket as a cartridge extractor; he can be trained to see shot in the air and advise his Gun accordingly, although he has the opportunity to do this only when there is not much shooting going on. But it is important that he really can see the shot and that he does not merely make hopeful comments which are no more than guesses. Seeing shot is a knack which can be learnt, but training is required. If you have a loader it will be worth while to take him to a shooting school with you, and if he claims to be able to see shot his ability can be tested by the instructor, and if he has never tried to see it he can learn how to do so, provided he is sufficiently alert and sharp eyed. On the subject of seeing shot, people sometimes ask, 'Why not use tracer?' The answer is that the indication of the tracer can be misleading. It is impossible for a shooter to see shot because of the smoke and hot gases coming out of the muzzle, which is why an observer must stand behind and look above the barrels; for the same reason the shooter cannot see tracer until it is well on its way to the target and possibly even beyond it. Tracer observed beyond a crossing target always gives an inaccurate impression of a miss behind even when the shot pattern was on the target. Furthermore, the tracer element rarely stays in the centre of the pattern and it may fly off to the extreme edge where it will be quite misleading. Tracer cartridges need careful testing before much faith can be placed in them, and accurate observation of their performance can only be achieved after training.

Safety is the most important element of shooting. Nearly everyone thinks he is safe, just as we all think we are good motor-car drivers: it is always the other fellow who is at fault. But a great many shooting men are unsafe at some time or another, even though they know the importance of safety and join in discussions about it. We all know that a gun should never be pointed at anyone whether it is loaded or not, but how often have you seen a group standing around chatting, guns under arms and muzzles pointing at each other's feet or at the dogs? A gun held under the upper arm and over the forearm should always be 'broken' so that all the world can see that it is unloaded, particularly when standing close to other people or when walking behind someone. Another safe way to carry a gun, walking or standing still, is over the shoulder, trigger guard uppermost and held at the grip; the trigger guard is kept up, not because if it were down the triggers might rub against the clothing at the shoulder and perhaps be operated, but because when it is up the bend of the stock results in the barrels pointing well up in the air, instead of nearly horizontal as is the case when the trigger guard is down.

Guns are sometimes pointed dangerously when walking-up. When you are expecting a shot you probably hold your gun in both hands, pointing forwards and up; be careful not to let the barrels sway back across your chest as you walk, because they may then point at the man on your left. Never hold a gun with both hands vertically down in front of the legs; the barrels are then horizontal and almost certain to be pointing dangerously, but this is an easy position adopted too often by lazy shooters while waiting for game.

Guns should always be unloaded before crossing a ditch or a fence and before putting them in a car or taking them into a house. If you are carrying an unloaded gun and you come to a fence, break the gun to see that it is unloaded before you climb over the fence; the same applies when you reach the car although you may know that you unloaded the gun ten minutes before. 'Unloaded' guns cause more accidents than those whose owners knew they were loaded.

Safe gun handling is a drill which should become automatic, so that the first thing you do when picking up a gun is to open it and make sure that it is unloaded; so that you never hand a gun to a friend, for instance, without first breaking it; so that you always unload at the end of a drive; so that you simply cannot hold a gun by its muzzles and pull it towards you, after crossing a fence or when taking it out of the car, for example.

Safety rules tend to be relaxed when shooting with only one or two companions, and the rough shooter or wild-fowler is inclined to have his gun loaded when he ought not to, because he is anxious not to miss the chance of a shot; it is better to be unloaded and miss an opportunity than to be loaded and wish, too late, that you had observed the rules of safety.

Remember that a shotgun can throw its pellets for two or three hundred yards and although they cannot penetrate much at that range they can damage an eye; and the rare phenomenon known as 'balling', when some of the pellets fuse together, could cause much more damage, even at long range. Balling sometimes occurs in an old gun whose latest owner is initially very pleased with an apparent bargain: 'Look at the barrels, old man, practically mirror smooth; jolly good condition isn't it?' But the old gun had heavily pitted barrels not long before and an unscrupulous dealer bored them out to remove the pits; as a result the barrels were made oversize, and when the gun was fired the cartridge wad could not fit properly to form an efficient seal, so that some of the flame from the exploding charge passed the wad and fused together clumps of the lead shot. Barrels in that condition can never throw a proper pattern and the buyer of such a gun would be lucky if he discovered the fault early, because he could easily be unaware of it unless he definitely tested the pattern on a plate, or even at home on a barn door; another less happy way of finding out about the balling would be by suddenly seeing a cow drop dead a couple of

70 Seeing the shot From this position a good loader can see the shot and he may be able to advise his Gun accordingly. Note the middle finger of the left hand straying across the barrel

hundred yards in front of the gun. The moral is to have a second-hand gun tested and fitted, and preferably before paying the full price. In the case of an over-bored gun the nature of the fault can only be discovered precisely by expert testing, with measurements taken along the inside of the barrels. This would be the first thing to do when a gun which 'looks perfect' produces patterns with evidence of balling.

Look up the barrels to see that they are clear after crawling through a hedge. Beware of ricochets, off hard ground or trees. Do not shoot unless you can see what lies beyond your target. Do not stand a gun upright against a car or tree or fence; it is dangerous because the gun can so easily be knocked over, perhaps by a dog, and it might go off if it was loaded, and also because a knock can dent the barrels.

Safety should be taught from the first time a gun is handled, and the younger the subject is, the better. There was a little boy and he had a little toy. . . . It was a pop-gun, firing a cork on a piece of string. He was 6 years old and his father told him never to point the gun at anyone. Many tears followed, for every time he was caught pointing the gun at someone, even by accident, it was taken from him and hung high up on a nail out of reach, and it was not returned to him until the next day. Father explained why it was dangerous to point a gun at people, especially a big gun like his, and that one day the boy might have a big gun too. On his 9th birthday the boy was given a garden gun which fired a small cartridge, and he learnt to use it to keep away marauding birds in the orchard. But sometimes he was caught handling his gun dangerously and then it was taken away for a week. When he was 12 a ·410 arrived and at first he carried it on shooting days, but without any cartridges. Later he was allowed to fire the gun, and the ultimate threat of removing it from him for the rest of the season for any breach of the safety rules never had to be put into effect. He grew up to a 12-bore and the big shooting days, and the drill he had learnt as a child ensured that he was always safe.

There are some who regret the passing nowadays of that sort of instruction to young people, or indeed to any not-so-young beginners, of the rules of shooting; make up your mind that no one will

71 Cheek off the stock   Did he hit it? It looks as if he took his cheek off the stock too soon. The grip of the left hand is good

catch you doing anything dangerous and that you too will be known as a Safe Gun.

A final matter of safety is a technical one and it concerns the Safety Catch. This name is misleading and so is the word 'Safe' which is revealed on most guns when the slide is in the rear position. The operation of this slide locks the triggers but that is all; it does not hold the action of the lock in any way. In an old gun the nose of the sear, where it engages in the tumbler bent, may be so worn that a sudden jar could cause it to slip off so that the tumbler, which is an internal hammer, is free to pivot under pressure from the mainspring and fire the gun. If the wood of the stock swells it does so inwards as well as outwards and this can prevent the sear from engaging properly in the bent; the jar of closing the gun could then cause the tumbler to slip free and fire the gun, and the same fault might be the reason for the second barrel going off unexpectedly when the first one is fired. Ordinary gun oil can cause the wood of a stock to swell and that is why you have been told to polish it only with linseed oil and a little turpentine.

Study Figure opposite for a description of how a box lock works and the effect of the safety catch.

In most guns the trigger lock is brought into position by the movement of the action lever when the gun is opened; this is called 'Automatic Safety', and if the gun is not so fitted the safety slide has to be moved back by hand after the gun has been closed. This is not very satisfactory and is a point to look for when you are buying an old second-hand gun, or certain foreign "Skeet" guns.

Side locks have an advantage over box locks because they usually incorporate an intercepting safety stop; if the tumbler is jarred away from the sear it cannot move far before it is held by this extra stop. But, although a normal side lock therefore embodies a means of preventing an accidental discharge due to the sear being jarred out of its position in the bent, this is not a 100 per cent certainty. In practice it has been found that a shock sufficient to jar the main tumbler sear out of the bent is also strong enough to jar the intercepting safety sear out of place, so that the intercepting safety stop cannot, after all, hold the tumbler and prevent the gun from firing. A top quality, London made best gun can, however, be fitted with a safety catch which locks the tumbler and is proof against jarring, but such guns are rare and expensive.

Figure 4 The limitation of the safety catch, and explanation of the main parts of a box lock

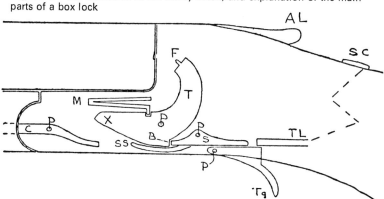

C — Cocking Lever. Its rear end pushes up the end of the Tumbler marked X when the gun is opened and the barrels drop down.

M — Mainspring. Here under stress, pushing against the Tumbler.

F — Firing pin, or Striker, which strikes the cap on the cartridge.

T — Tumbler, which is in fact the hammer.

B — Bent, bearing against the nose of the Sear.

SS — Sear spring. Trying to push the front end of the Sear, its nose, upwards.

S — Sear, in contact with the upper part, the blade, of the Trigger.

P — Pivots, round which can move the Cocking Lever, Tumbler, Sear and Trigger.

Tg — Trigger.

TL — Trigger Lock. Actuated by the Action Lever in an 'Automatic Safety' lock, it slides forward and prevents the Trigger blade from being raised, and so locks the Trigger.

AL — Action Lever. Opens the gun. Called a top lever when it is on top of the gun, its most usual position.

SC — Safety Catch. When moved forward it brings the Trigger Lock back, free of the Trigger blade. The actual mechanism is not shown.

Note that in a double-barrelled gun most of these parts are repeated.

Method of Firing

1 The gun is now cocked and the safety catch is on.
2 Moving the Safety Catch forward slides the Trigger Lock back.
3 Pressing the Trigger pushes up the back end of the Sear.
4 The Sear nose at the front then dips down and slips off the Bent of the Tumbler.
5 The Mainspring exerts pressure on the Tumbler which pivots, so that the firing pin jumps forward into the hole in the breech and fires the cartridge.

N.B. The Safety Catch only locks the Trigger, and in a worn gun the pressure of the Mainspring can be sufficient to push the Bent off the nose of the Sear, particularly if the gun is jarred; the Tumbler is then free to pivot and fire the cartridge.

While considering the workings of a lock you might reflect on the accuracy needed to adjust trigger pulls. The work consists of filing the tumbler bent and sear nose so that they slide apart on the appropriate amount of pressure being applied to the trigger. This is skilful craftsmanship and the job should not be entrusted to a gun dealer who has not the services of a proper gunsmith.

Mention was made a few paragraphs back of the rules of shooting. The rules are less strictly adhered to now than they used to be 50 years ago, when it was not uncommon for the culprit to be ordered home forthwith after some mistake which broke the rules. All the same, there is a certain etiquette of the shooting field whose observation makes life easier for everyone concerned.

Be careful to shoot only your own birds and do not try for those which are flying towards one of the other Guns; err on the generous side rather than the greedy. Do not criticize other people's misses, nor boast about your own kills. If you have an unruly dog keep it under control even if that means tethering it during a drive, and never comment on the bad behaviour of other dogs, more especially if you have no dog of your own; the Gun with the bad dog is at least trying, probably, and having no dog yourself you are really only half equipped for the job in hand. Be ready with your praise for good shooting, or a smart bit of dogwork, and if you should fire at a bird at the same time as someone else give him the credit for having killed it: tip your hat to him and make some complimentary remark like 'Your bird, Sir!' or 'Good shot!' even though you may be almost certain that you shot the bird.

Do not talk or make a noise when game is near, particularly partridges, and keep a total in your head of the birds you shoot during a drive. You should especially note the birds which are runners and see that action is taken to find them after the drive, either with your own dog or the picker-up's, or by informing the 'keeper. Try to be fair about this, especially if you are not shooting well and have but a small number of birds down. Hosts and 'keepers and dog-men soon know the Gun who always has a 'bird hard hit over by that hedge,' which turns out to be the cause of a time-wasting search for a quite unharmed pheasant. You may not be aware of the fact that a pheasant which has cleared the Guns very often starts to glide down towards its selected cover, and if you turn round and shoot at it at that moment you may be misled, on seeing it start to glide, into thinking you have hit it. Watch for the bird dropping a leg down and be honest with yourself, and others, about claiming purely imaginary and plaintively hopeful hits that are really quite obvious misses.

Sometimes in September young pheasants are shot in mistake for partridges. They ought not to be because a pheasant's wing shape is different from a partridge's and the beat is slower. If you fall into this error no one will mind very much if you own up and apologize, but do not try to conceal your crime.

Shooting is for sport, and rough shooting and wild-fowling wholly so, apart from the fact that the results are good to eat. But when game is reared and driven the expenses are considerable, so that the shooter has a responsibility to his host, or to the syndicate if he is a member; there is a real need to obtain a good bag which can be sold to offset the cost of the shoot. While a good shot is likely to receive more invitations to shoot because of his skill, he may still find himself somewhat left out in the cold if he breaks the rules of conduct. The average shot who is keen and pleasant company and who knows how to behave is always welcome, and after all, by definition, most shooting men are average shots.

You can inspire faith in your regard for safety if you have your gun open when you walk about with it over your forearm. Watch this point next time you go shooting and see what your opinions are of those who do carry their guns broken and of those others whose gun barrels are frequently pointing at the feet of their companions. A proper shooting man automatically experiences an inward mistrust and worry when he sees a gun held barrels down and, as the owner turns to talk to his neighbour, the barrels point at a dog and then at someone else's legs, even if the observer is fairly sure that the gun is not loaded.

Always ensure that you know where your neighbouring Guns are, and if they are round a corner or over a hedge, walk round until you can locate them exactly. This applies as much as when rough shooting or waiting for roosting pigeon as it does when on an organized driven shoot. When you are given a numbered peg for a drive you can assume that it is the best place for you to stand, and that there is, therefore, no point in you edging forward or to one side if the first birds to appear seem to warrant a change in your position. If, for some exceptional reason you wish to change your position, and the reason must be serious, such as an angry bull, you *must* inform the nearby Guns. If you do not it will be your fault if you are shot, although that is poor consolation for the unfortunate fellow who fired the shot. It is more likely that no harm will result from your moving from your allotted place, except that you will gain a reputation of being 'A greedy so-and-so who won't stay where he is put.'

If you are walking with the beaters remember that your job is to deal with birds which break back; those that go forward are not yours, and they should be left to the main line of Guns.

At the end of the day, speak well of it. Do not moan and complain if you are wet and cold and the rain has resulted in only a small bag. Remember that the 'keepers and beaters have been out far longer than you have and are a good deal more wet and tired. Always have a word with the head gamekeeper before you go, congratulate him on a good day and sympathize with him after a poor one, and let him know that you have enjoyed yourself. If you have not you had better give up shooting. Be generous when you tip the head 'keeper, because his reward is not only for services rendered on that particular day but on all the days of the year, and because he works exceptionally long hours and is a dedicated man without whose help the shooting of driven game in any quantity would cease.

A most important responsibility of all shooters is that of causing the minimum suffering to the creatures they kill. If you live in a town you may be unable to keep a dog, but if you live in the country and wish to shoot you ought at least to investigate carefully the possibility of having a gundog; training it, to a reasonable standard, is interesting and not particularly difficult or, if you can pay the price, you can obtain a trained dog. Only with a dog will you be doing your utmost to increase the bag on a shooting day, and to retrieve wounded game which might otherwise escape to die slowly.

You should know how to kill wounded game. For a bird, the neatest method is to hold it with your thumb under its chin, forefinger behind its head, turn the hand over so that the bird hangs down with its breast away from you, and then give it a sharp flick downwards which will break its neck. The art of this method lies in knowing precisely how strong a flick to give, according to the weight and toughness of the bird; if you use the same strength on a young partridge that might be needed for an old cock pheasant

---

72 **Most things wrong**   Weight on right leg, cheek right off stock, heavy grip with left hand and not far enough out along the barrels which are canted over to the right

you will find the bird's head in your hand and a decapitated corpse on the ground. An easier and equally effective method is to grasp the bird with both hands, breast uppermost and with its wings held in to its body, and then to rap the back of its head smartly on the toe of your boot or on a tree or post. Do not use your gun as a club and try to beat the creature to death; this extra-ordinary performance is quite frequently carried out by inexperi-enced shooters who are justifiably anxious to end the suffering of some beast they have shot, particularly a hare or rabbit. Very often the result is a broken gun stock.

To kill a hare, pick it up by the small of its back, not by its back legs, and chop it sharply with the edge of your hand across the back of its neck. The same method will deal with a rabbit although, as the animal is so much weaker, you can also use the same left hand grip and break its neck by putting your right hand across the back of the neck and pushing down and away from you.

Finally, try to avoid being a nuisance to others. Be self-con-tained so that you do not have to borrow cartridges, a mackintosh, the services of a dog or cash for the tip at the end of the day. Be cheerful and look as though you are enjoying yourself and you will then give pleasure to others also.

10 Practice

Repetition is inevitable in any instruction. If you become a little weary of being told to practise you should try to accept the fact that only if you do actively and physically practise what you are asked to do will you be able to become a good shot. Practice in the shooting field is limited to a few months of the year, but it is possible to keep your hand in, and learn, and gain experience at any time. Merely reading about the correct drill in a book is not sufficient.

Clay pigeon shooting provides good practice, provided you understand its limitations when applied to game shooting. Competitive clay shooting, for its own sake, is a specialist subject and the technique is different from that required for live birds.

Apart from the big national and international clay-shooting competitions there are numerous small events organized by local gun clubs throughout the country, and if you attend some of these, you will have an excellent opportunity to study style: some fair, some very good and some really bad. If you compete you can gain experience of shooting in company and of being watched by other people, and you ought to be able to overcome any nervousness in this respect.

Skeet is a particular form of clay shooting where the traps are in two towers in front of the shooter, who fires at a 'bird' from each tower from several positions on the circumference of a semicircle whose diameter is a line drawn between the two towers. Details of the rules and scoring will not be given here; suffice it to say that in normal Skeet the shooting is done from a 'gun down' position and not with the gun held at the shoulder, and it therefore can be beneficial to gun mounting and quick swinging. It will also show you that plenty of other people can miss clays.

In Down The Line shooting, or DTL as it is called, the gun is held at the shoulder and the shooter calls to the trapper that he is ready for the clay bird to be released. This unnatural method might be scorned by those who consider they are only interested in real shooting, but even they can learn something from it. When you try DTL you will find that it teaches you to have the butt properly into your shoulder; if you put the gun up and the butt is not bedded correctly you have time to sense the wrong attitude, to lower the gun and to mount it again before you call for the clay to be released. When you do shoot you will find that you have to do so quickly, with your cheek well on to the stock, and the concentration that is required for every shot will again help to remove the anxiety arising from being watched.

The most interesting form of trapshooting is the game layout, which many small clubs possess and which is found in a more elaborate and comprehensive state at a Shooting School. The 'game' represented can be walked-up partridges or driven grouse, a running rabbit or a springing teal and high birds, 40 yards up, which you can consider as pheasants or geese according to taste. On a good game layout, traps can be sprung while you are walking, and clays can be sent at you over trees and also in bunches of four or more at a time, so that you can practise gun mounting under a variety of conditions and also picking a bird out of a covey. The clays can be sent off in a variety of different angles, and at unexpected times so that the shooter is confronted with targets that give a good representation of the real thing.

A simple and inexpensive form of clay shooting can be arranged on any local piece of open ground by using a hand flinger. This is a form of sling from which clays can be thrown without the need for a comparatively expensive trap, and two or three friends shooting and throwing in turn can have an amusing afternoon's sport. With a hand flinger and permission to shoot in a field where it is safe to do so, you can get your eye in before the season starts and without having to visit the grounds of a club or school.

As a matter of general practice you should pick up your gun as often as you can, which is a good reason for keeping it in a handy cupboard and not dismantled in a case. Hold the gun in both hands, get the feel of it, and mount it at some object you can see

---

73 Lessons from a club clay shoot   A visit to any gun club's clay-pigeon shoot will reveal some remarkable styles to the student. This is a good stance, a long left reach and the smoke shows that the shot has been taken so that there is an excuse for the cheek being off the stock

through the window. Better still, take the gun outside into the garden or put it in the car and drive out to the country. Put the muzzles on a starling or any other bird that appears and swing out in front of it and say, 'Bang!' to yourself when you would have fired, or use snap caps, if you have them, and actually pull the trigger on these practice shots. Try to check where the gun is pointing as you 'fire', but do not stop the swing and do not look specifically at the barrels. Find some telegraph wires or overhead electric cables and take up your stance in front of them; put the muzzles on while your body pivots and carries them along, and see that the muzzles remain on the line while the gun is being mounted, so that they never deviate from the line until well after the shot would have been taken. The sequence of this action is:

1 Body starts first to move along the line on which you are going to shoot.
2 Left hand connects the muzzles to the line.
3 Left hand holds the muzzles securely on the line while the body continues to pivot and the butt is raised to meet the shoulder.

When you can do this drill accurately you will feel certain, as you pull the trigger, that you are right on the target and that had it been a real bird you would surely have killed it.

Practise your footwork, too, for the shot taken behind and for shooting on rough ground or on a slope. Just as the golfer practises his swing and the cricketer spends time at the nets, so the shooter needs to train his muscles to act exactly as he requires them, smoothly and without any strain or any delay. Look again at Photograph 55. Can you adopt this position easily, quickly and surely? If not, you ought to train yourself to be able to do so. Remember to practise swing and body pivoting in a restricted position, when kneeling or sitting; take your gun out of the cupboard and do it there, in the room.

If you really want to be a good shot you must train your body accordingly, and you must take steps to keep in form when you are not able to do much game shooting. Three ways of doing this are by exercises, by pigeon shooting and by clay shooting.

Rifle shots do exercises to strengthen their wrists and arms in order to be the better able to hold a steady aim. Shotgun users need to practise movement and co-ordination between their eyes and the rest of their bodies; the following exercises will help you to train your body to follow the dictates of your brain.

74 Lessons from a club clay shoot The inexperienced novice who has not yet been taught. Weight right back, left heel raised; butt not properly in shoulder; cheek right away from stock; bad left hand grip, on the fore-end instead of out along barrels. But the amused look on his face shows that he thinks it is fun; he has every chance of being a good shot one day

Exercises

1 Adopt the ready position for shooting, butt under the right forearm, left hand loosely holding the barrels just in front of the fore-end, left forefinger extended towards the muzzles, gun barrels pointing up at about 45°. Run your left hand forward along the barrels as you put the muzzles on any convenient object in front of you at about head height. Mount the gun slowly, allowing the barrels to slide through the fingers of the left hand, forwards and then very slightly backwards. When the butt is at your shoulder grip the barrels with your left thumb and fingers. The exercise emphasizes the need for a loose hold with the left hand in the early stages so that the barrels can *slide* through it as the stock is raised. If you grip firmly with your left hand when you first put the muzzles on you will probably find that raising the butt results in the muzzles tipping down slightly, so that they are off the target and you have to push them up again. The muzzles must not wave up and down like that, but they often will unless you can make your left hand allow the barrels to slip through it and only nip them firmly when the gun is at your shoulder.

2 Mount the gun at some mark slightly above the horizontal. Take away your left hand and hold the muzzles on the mark. This shows how the grip of your right hand must be firmly locked on to the small of the butt, and how it also holds the butt well into your shoulder, which should also be bearing forward against the butt. Do this several times and check that you have taken a firm hold with your right hand and placed the butt correctly, into your shoulder; if you have not done so it will be apparent when you take your left hand off the barrels.

3 Choose a mark in front of you and one each side at rather more than a right angle from your front. Bring the gun up at each mark in turn, pivoting the body round so that your chest remains obliquely to the direction in which the gun points. Do not let your arms swing across your body, keep leaning forward, weight on your left foot and right heel clear of the ground. The heel should swing to right and left as your body pivots and when you have the

75 **Lessons from a club clay shoot** A high bird for this automatic user. His stance is too wide, weight too far back, cheek off stock *at* the moment of firing: you can see the spent cartridge being ejected out of the side of the breech. Incidentally, he is wearing one of the cartridge belts with narrow loops, described in Chapter 2 and not recommended.

gun well round to the left your right heel ought to be almost as far off the ground as is a golfer's at the end of a drive. Keep your left leg stiff and the rest of your body supple. Swing slowly at first and then speed up the gun mounting, and beware of dropping your weight back on to your right foot when you point to the mark on the right-hand side.

4   Look at Photograph 36. Practise that overhead shot. Reach forward with the gun, think to yourself, 'Up!' and try to put the gun as near as possible to your imaginary target. Keep the left foot firm and allow the right heel to rise. Swing to the perpendicular and a little beyond, but remind yourself that you actually took the shot a little before the gun became vertical. Tell yourself that you must not lean back on to the right foot, for that would mean pulling the muzzles back, down away from your bird and you are trying to reach up and up, as far as you can. Do this exercise until you have the feel of the sway forward and until you are confident that you have lost any tendency to want to drop back on to your right foot.

5   Repeat the exercises from a kneeling and from a sitting position. When you can do them effortlessly you will be certain of increasing the number of your kills when you are shooting from an awkward position, in a pigeon hide or when wildfowling.

Do you shoot pigeon? If not, you should. Too many game shots do not bother with the humble pigeon but if they did they would become better shots. Apart from the fact that pigeon can be shot all the year round, thus providing live practice during the summer months, they can also be remarkably difficult to hit. If you can knock down pigeon you will not find it difficult to hit 'ordinary' pheasants, which are the ones that make up the greater proportion of the bag; the high pheasants and the curling ones are the exceptions that are talked about and remembered but the ordinary ones provide reasonably simple, fast moving, straight flying shots. Perhaps you have other interests during the summer and your spare time is fully occupied with tennis or golf or gardening, fishing or sailing or simply being domesticated with the family. All the same, if you take advantage of harvest time, when pigeon can usually be shot over decoys, you will be in better form for your game shooting than if you have never fired a gun since the end of the previous season.

76 A pigeon shooter's bag Pigeon shooter's bag after an afternoon on August stubble. Twenty-nine birds, and some useful practice before the game-shooting season starts

77 A pigeon-shooter's hide A pigeon-shooting hide. Shooter wears face veil

78 Pigeon decoys Part of a layout, including a real bird mounted on a stick. At least twenty decoys are needed, and preferably more

The third method of learning about shooting if you are a beginner, or keeping in form if you are a reasonably accomplished shot, is to practise on clay pigeons. We have already discussed the competitive shooting organized by gun clubs but the way to learn as well as to practise is to visit a Shooting School. The cost of such a visit may seem expensive, but it is mostly made up of the price of the clays and the cartridges and no one who has good, practical instruction from a coach who knows his job ever regrets the price he paid for it. All shooters have faults or develop them sooner or later and a Shooting School instructor can see them after only a few shots. You can learn something by watching a good shot in the field: you can marvel at his easy, confident style and perhaps try to emulate it, but it is unlikely that you will learn much by asking him what he does or how he does it. A good performer is but rarely a good instructor as well. Furthermore, a naturally good shot is likely to be a poor instructor because he finds shooting easy and cannot understand other people's difficulties, and because he is unable to analyse correctly his own actions, and if pressed for information he may well give advice contrary to the manner in which he obtains his excellent results. Good shooting coaches are not natural shots, but they have learnt to be very good shots, and they have also acquired a store of knowledge of all the many ways in which their pupils can follow strange impulses to do the wrong thing. Coaches are also used to seeing many more clays missed than hit and there is no need for a pupil to be shy about putting up a poor performance. Consistent missing, in fact, is usually cured fairly easily and it is the inconsistent shot who requires especially careful diagnosis of his faults.

You can visit a Shooting School for specific instruction if you are a beginner, although if you have read this book *and acted* on what you have been told you ought not to need much basic teaching. Or you can visit the school to check faults and improve if you are off form. Very likely you will not know your fault but merely be only too aware of its result: usually continually missing a particular shot, a partridge going away to the left, a pheasant crossing to the right, or whatever it is. The fault may be due to increasing age, when reflexes have slowed, muscles have stiffened and weight has increased; none of these physical changes need stop you shooting but they can require adjustment in the fit of your gun, and the need for this will be apparent to the instructor as soon as he sees you shoot.

Many of the clients of the shooting schools are regulars whose normal shooting companions would consider them as being beyond the need for lessons; they are the consistently good shots whose performance is always admired, but they are also very much aware of the need to keep in practice and to find their form again during the late summer before the new season starts. No one should attend a big day at the beginning of a shooting season without some practice beforehand, at pigeon or at clays, and the best way of doing this, with a professional at hand to ensure that faults are not being perpetuated, is to go to a Shooting School.

The instructor can see the shot, so that he can tell where you are shooting, and he can present the types of targets that will show up your weaknesses and do you most good. He will also know various ranges on the ground and the heights of the trees and the towers which hold the traps for the high birds, so you will be tested on your ability to judge distance as well.

A fault that a shooting coach can see at once is a tendency to flinch and this is more common than might be supposed. Indeed, it has been suggested that one of the causes of the universal tendency to slow down the swing just at the critical moment when, if anything, it ought to be speeded up, is a quick, involuntary flinch when the brain tells the finger to pull the trigger; the anticipation of the noise and shock of the explosion causes this disastrous hesitation. Flinching is much more common in young and inexperienced shots and among those whose guns do not fit them, but sometimes it can develop in a man who has done a good deal of shooting; it is usually caused by some physical shock, such as a sore shoulder or headache as a result of firing an unusual number of cartridges, but the victim may be unaware of the flinch and may never realize its existence until some outside observer spots it and tells him about it. The real cure for flinching, once the patient is aware of what he is doing, is courage and determination to overcome it; this may not be easy, like giving up smoking, but it can be made a little easier in bad cases by improving the fit of the gun and confidence can be restored by letting the victim shoot a number of rounds with a gun that makes very little noise and recoil, perhaps a ·410 or even a ·22 rifle. Later, the shooter may graduate back to full bore and load by way of a 16-bore, or a 12-bore and 2-inch cartridges. Flinching is fatal to good shooting. It can be overcome with experience and encouragement, once it has been identified as the cause of the poor results; if the temperament of the shooter does not allow it to be overcome he will never be a good shot.

Once upon a time there was a young man who decided to take up shooting and to treat the matter seriously. He read a book about it. He became interested and read several more books. He bought a gun and most of the equipment he had read about, such as cartridge bag and belt and clothes and boots and hat, and then he began looking around for a shoot. In the meantime, fortunately, he went to a Shooting School. He took his new gun out of its unmarked case, dumped half a dozen books on the table and said to the instructor, 'I've read all those, and now I want to do some shooting!'

The instructor took his client, who evidently did not consider himself a pupil, round some of the stands and after several shots had been fired at simple going-away targets, and at driven partridges and overhead pheasants without a clay being broken, the young man asked his first question. 'What's the matter?' said he. 'I'm not hitting anything, and the only result is that I've got a sore shoulder.'

The comment from the instructor was: 'I'm glad you've asked a question at last, Sir. But I cannot agree about your sore shoulder as you have not yet put the gun there. You have been shooting off the top of your arm.'

Asked for further explanation the coach pointed out that although the shooter had read several books he had not been doing any of the things they had told him: his stance was wrong, his gun mounting was hopeless and his swing non-existent. Perhaps he would like to go back to the first stand and start again? 'No thanks,' replied the young man. 'I'm too darned sore. But I'd like to come again in a week or two.'

'Right,' said the instructor. 'And please read your books again, carefully. Deal with each subject separately and practise as you go along. Read about stance and then stand up and put your feet in the positions described. When the book describes gun mounting or swinging, pick up your gun and follow what the book says. Get the feel of leaning forward on the left foot, of thrusting out the left arm, of hugging the butt into your shoulder and the stock against your cheek. You cannot learn about shooting by sitting down and reading a book; you must practise the details, step by step.'

On his next visit the young man was somewhat chastened. 'I thought I knew a good deal about it when I came last time,' he admitted. 'But now I have been practising what the books say and I feel I know very little, but I would like to try a few shots.'

He fired 100 cartridges, scored a fair number of kills and was delighted, particularly as he had no sore arm at the end. From then on he continued to make progress and he read his books with more understanding because he made the effort, while he was reading, to get up and take his gun and go through the motions described in the instruction.

You can guess the moral of this story? Then please, if you wish to benefit from *this* book, having read it, studied the illustrations and gained a few ideas, read the specifically instructional parts again with your gun in your hands and physically *do* what you are asked to.

Methods of teaching shooting, although they all have the same object, may differ slightly. If you are shooting with success do not change your style merely because someone else says he shoots in a certain way. But if you are not really successful, and that applies to the majority of shooters, adopt the methods advocated here, and persevere, and your shooting will improve.

Good and experienced shots sometimes develop apparently inexplicable faults which cause them to miss certain birds. Even if they explain to themselves the reasons for missing, the chances are that they will be wrong and only a coach who can watch them in action will be able to find the real cause. Here are some examples.

A very good shot, who justifiably prided himself on his ability to kill pheasants coming straight overhead, began to miss them. He tried to swing further ahead but all his efforts were of no avail and finally he decided that there must be something wrong with his eyes. He made up his mind to consult an oculist. Shortly before his appointment to have his eyes tested he visited a Shooting School where 10 clays were sent over him from the pheasant tower; he missed them all. In despair he turned to the instructor and said, 'I feel I shall never kill an overhead bird again!'

'That's not true,' said his coach. 'You'll kill the next 10 if you just do one thing I ask you. Keep your cheek on the stock until after the shot, and check that it really is there.'

The next 10 clays were all hit. 'Amazing!' exclaimed the shooter. 'I can scarcely believe I've been so foolish. I have travelled 90 miles to find out that, but it's worth it. And I thought my eyesight was wrong. . . .'

Most of these troubles that creep into shooting can be cured quite simply, and if you suffer from one you ought to be able to trace it, if you read carefully about the particular shot which worries you and analyse all your actions compared with the correct drill.

There was an expert grouse shooter whose skill was a joy to see. He loved his moors and his birds but he rarely did much pheasant shooting, and had no experience of high birds. One year he came south at the end of the season and was persuaded by a friend to join a cocks-only day. He did not expect to do particularly well as he knew the pheasants would be fast and high but he thought he would enjoy himself. At the first stand he had a few shots and failed to connect. The same thing happened at subsequent stands,

---

79 Lessons from a club clay shoot   He looks confident as he swings on to his second clay, having broken the first

much to his dismay. For the last drive his friend came and stood with him and watched the first bird missed. 'You're miles behind,' said the friend. 'When you come up on your bird, give your gun a good flick forward.'

Our grouse shooter did this flick and the next bird dropped dead. So did the next three, and that was the end of the day and of the season. But at the start of the next season, when he confidently took his place in a grouse butt, he was astonished to find that he missed most of the birds. He took his trouble to his usual shooting instructor who asked him to demonstrate on low incoming clays, and promptly said: 'You have developed an extraordinary flick up with the gun. I don't know why, you've never done it before.' Having been told this the shooter settled down to his normal style and soon he was hitting every clay. Then he told his coach about those last pheasants at the end of the previous season, and how he had been told to flick up his gun.

The moral of this one is that you should not adopt 'patent cures', somebody's bright idea, which will probably result in you falling into a bad habit which will ruin the rest of your shooting. The expert grouse shooter merely lacked the experience, and the picture in his mind, of giving the extra forward allowance necessary for tall pheasants. Personal analysis of his actions and the correct method of dealing with an oncoming bird could have showed him his error; as it was, his instructor spotted the fault at once.

Another complaint brought to a shooting coach was from a client who said he nearly always missed driven partridges when they came to his left. He was a good shot and when confronted with the driven partridge stand at the school he killed most of the clays that went over his head or to his right, but he failed on those to the left. He missed them all behind.

'Take up your position ready to shoot,' said the instructor. 'Now, see how the gun barrels are pointing across your body to the left. When you take a clay in front or to your right you put the muzzles on correctly and swing up and through it. But when the target is on your left, because your barrels are already pointing in that direction you just bring them straight up and fire *at* the bird.'

The pupil looked interested and his teacher went on: 'Hold the gun so that the barrels point to your front. Put the muzzles on and I know you will hit the next clay.'

80 The shooting school   A pair of clays over the shooter at the school

The trap was set to throw clays to the shooter's left and he broke the next clay and half a dozen more in a row: a simple cure for a simple fault.

You have been told that when you miss you will almost certainly do so behind. It is possible to miss in front, but only just, in exceptional circumstances, as the following tale shows.

An elderly gentleman of considerable shooting experience had been a very good shot but found that he was becoming worse and worse. He missed so much that he decided to consult a coach before finally giving up shooting. 'I'm missing everything behind,' he explained. 'I just can't catch up with them any more. Can you help me?'

This is a common enough fault but the instructor could hardly believe his eyes when his client started shooting. Every miss was in front. When he was told this the shooter maintained that it could not be true. 'Well, Sir,' replied the instructor, 'I can see the shot a yard or sometimes more in front of the clay. Just try reducing your lead by about half.'

Success was immediate, and consistent for several more clays. 'I can hardly believe it,' said the shooter. 'But you are obviously right. I almost feel I ought to sack my faithful loader, who has been with me for years.'

'Why?' asked the coach.

'Well, I've been missing almost everything I shot at and always my loader says, "You're be'ind 'im, Sir. You're be'ind 'im." I suppose he meant to be helpful. . . .'

So it can be done, this missing in front, but it is most unusual. You will doubtless agree that it is unwise to accept advice about where your shots are going from a loader or anyone else unles you are certain he can see the shot, no matter how much faith you have in him on other matters.

Learn all you can about shooting if you want to extract full enjoyment from it. Read other books which deal with natural history and game rearing and the management of shoots. Learn the language of the sport so that, for example, you do not talk of a bag of '53 brace of pheasant'. Two dead pheasants are called a brace but more are numbered, so that '53 brace' is correctly termed '106'. And if you walk the fields in the spring you will not see 'a brace of partridge' fly over the hedge, but 'a pair of partridges'. Watch the style of better shots than yourself and study shooting photographs in illustrated magazines; when you criticize, to yourself, the faults of others, be sure that you also pass judgement on your own performance. The object of this book is to help you to shoot straighter, but remember that it is better to be a safe sportsman than to be an expert cad.

APPENDIX A
Notes on the Protection of Birds Acts 1954 and 1967

1 Game birds excluded

The Acts do not apply to game birds which are listed as follows: pheasant, partridge, grouse, black game and in Scotland, ptarmigan. The Game Act of 1831 caters for game birds.

2 General protection

All wild birds are protected unless named in the Acts in the list of birds which may be shot; the Acts prescribe the period of the shooting season for each bird in that list. The shooting seasons are, with the exception of the season for woodcock, applicable in all counties of England, Scotland and Wales.

3 Shooting on Sundays and on Christmas Day

The Acts prohibit the shooting of any wild bird in Scotland on Sundays and on Christmas Day.

Regarding England and Wales there is no such prohibition, but the Acts give power to the Home Secretary to prohibit shooting on Sundays in any county. If in doubt as to the position in your county, ask your local council or police.

4 Decoys

It is an offence under the Acts to use as a decoy any live bird which is tethered or which is secured by means of braces or other similar appliances, or which is blind, maimed or injured.

5 Use of boats

The Acts make it illegal to use 'any mechanically propelled vehicle, boat or any aircraft in immediate pursuit of a wild bird for the purpose of driving, killing or taking that bird'.

6   List of birds which may be shot and the respective shooting seasons

1 October– 31 January   *12 August–31 January*
Capercaillie   Common Snipe

Inland: 1 September–31 January
Foreshore: 1 September–20 February

(*Foreshore is defined in the Acts as 'in or over any area below high-water mark of ordinary spring tides'.*)

Common Pochard	Pintail	Wild geese –
Gadwall	Shoveler	Canada
Goldeneye	Teal	Greylag
Mallard	Tufted duck	Pinkfoot
	Wigeon	

1 September–31 January

Coot
Golden Plover
Moorhen

In Scotland: 1 September–31 January
In England and Wales: 1 October–31 January

Woodcock

7   List of birds which may be shot at any time of the year by an authorized person

Carrion Crow	Lesser Black-backed Gull
Collared Dove	Herring Gull
Domestic pigeon gone wild	Jackdaw
Hooded Crow	Rook
Magpie	Starling
Jay	Wood-pigeon
House Sparrow	
Greater Black-backed Gull	

Note:

(*a*) Under the Acts an 'authorized person' is the landowner, tenant or person having the sporting rights, or a person having permission from one of these three; or any person authorized in writing by the local authority or by certain statutory bodies such as the Nature Conservancy, river boards and local fishery committees.

(*b*) The shooting season for game birds, which may only be shot by holders of a game licence, are as follows, both days inclusive:
Pheasant – 1 October to 1 February
Partridge – 1 September to 1 February
Grouse – 12 August to 10 December
Blackgame – 20 August to 10 December
Ptarmigan – 12 August to 10 December

Copies of the Acts may be obtained from HM Stationery Office or through most booksellers.

(*c*) A Game Licence is required before shooting Snipe, Woodcock and also Hares.

(*d*) Amendments are continually being made by which species are changed from one Schedule to another so that, for example, oystercatchers, bullfinches and ravens may now be shot in certain areas. Also, bird sanctuaries are defined, and orders are made prohibiting Sunday shooting in certain counties.

(*e*) Many species which formerly could legitimately be shot are now protected under the Wildlife and Countryside Act 1981.

APPENDIX B

Organizations concerned with shooting and sources of information

British Field Sports Society (BFSS) Director: Maj. Gen. J. O. C. R. Hopkinson, 59 Kennington Road, London, S.E.1.
Works for the furtherance of all field sports, particularly combating propaganda issued by organizations opposed to them. Also issues excellent explanatory pamphlets for young people and can inform members where sport may be obtained.

Clay Pigeon Shooting Association (CPSA) Secretary: A. P. Page, 107 Epping New Road, Buckhurst Hill, Essex.

Controls clay shooting throughout Great Britain and organizes national championships. Can supply information about local clubs, most of which are affiliated to it.

The Game Conservancy Secretary: H. Smith-Carington, Fordingbridge, Hants.

Carries out scientific research and practical investigations into factors influencing the survival and numbers of game in the British Isles. Provides an advisory and information service on game production and management. Produces a range of advisory booklets and instructional films.

British Association for Shooting and Conservation (BASC) Director: Lt-Cdr J. W. Anderson, Marford Mill, Rossett, Clwyd.

WAGBI assists wildfowlers, protects their rights and organizes rearing and ringing of wildfowl. Many local gun clubs, even inland ones not concerned with 'fowling, are affiliated to it. Help is given to members seeking information about shooting areas, especially where the foreshore rights belong to a local club.

The Field
Carmelite House, Carmelite Street, London EC4

Articles on most sports, including shooting. Useful advertisements for dogs, guns, shoots, etc.

Shooting Times & Country Magazine
10 Sheet Street, Windsor, Berks.

Articles on all aspects of shooting. News of BASC, BFSS and CPSA.

The Gun Code

Notes on safety, behaviour, game seasons, etc. Should be read by everyone on obtaining his first gun. From the British Field Sports Society.

Eley Shotgun Cartridges for Game and Wildfowl Shooting

Describes cartridges, loads, shot sizes available, etc. From Eley, PO Box 216, Witton, Birmingham.

Wild Birds and the Law

Details of which are protected and when. From the Royal Society for the Protection of Birds, The Lodge, Sandy, Beds.

Notes on the Proof of Shotguns and Other Small Arms

Types of proof, foreign proof marks, black powder, magnum cartridges, sale of guns, buying second-hand guns. From The Proof House, Banbury Street, Birmingham.

APPENDIX C
Notes on the Firearms Act 1968

Airguns

A person under 17 but over 14 may not buy any air weapon but he may borrow one or be given one. He may use it without supervision.

A person under 14 may only be in possession of an airgun when he is under the supervision of someone older than 21.

Shotguns

A shotgun certificate, obtainable from the police, is required in order to possess a shotgun.

A person under 17 but over 15 may not buy but may borrow or be given a gun and use it without supervision, provided he holds a shotgun certificate.

A person under 15 may not own a gun but may use one under the supervision of someone older than 21.

These notes are very brief. Foi further details see *A Summary of the Law relating to the Possession and Use of Firearms and Ammunition*, which can be obtained from The Gun Trade Association, 22 Park Gate Road, Cannock Wood, Rugely, Staffs.

APPENDIX D
Shotgun certificates and game licences

1 Gun licences have been abolished. Since May 1968, Shotgun Certificates have taken their place.
2 In order to possess a shotgun, a certificate must be obtained from the police, who provide the application form. The certificate costs £12 and is valid for three years.
3 A game licence is required to shoot game (see notes to Appendix A) The licence costs £6 and lasts from 1 August until 31 July the following year. A shortened period from 1 August to 31 October or from 1 November to 31 July costs £4. For any consecutive fourteen days the fee is £2. A gamekeeper's licence costs £4 for a year.
4 Game may not be shot on Sundays or on Christmas Day.

APPENDIX E
Bibliography

'BB', *The Shooting Man's Bedside Book*, Eyre & Spottiswoode.

BRANDER, MICHAEL, *The International Encyclopedia of Shooting*, Pelham, 1972.

BRANDER, MICHAEL, *The Rough Shooter's Dog*, Gentry, 1971.

BURRARD, SIR GERALD, *In the Gunroom*.

BURRARD, SIR GERALD, *The Modern Shotgun*, vol. 1: *The Gun*, vol. 2: *The Cartridge*, vol. 3: *The Gun and the Cartridge*.

CARLISLE, G. L., *Grouse and Gun*, Stanley Paul, 1983.

CARLISLE, G. L., and STANBURY, PERCY, *Shotgun and Shooter*, Barrie & Jenkins, 1981.

COATES, ARCHIE, *Amateur Keeper*.

COATES, ARCHIE, *Pigeon Shooting*, André Deutsch, 1970.

COLES, CHARLES, *Shooting and Stalking*, Stanley Paul, 1983.

CRUDGINGTON, I. M., and BAKER, D. J., *The British Shotgun*, vol. 1, Barrie & Jenkins, 1978.

ERLANDSON, KEITH, *Gundog Training*, Barrie & Jenkins, 1976.

GARWOOD, G. T., *Gough Thomas's Gun Book*, Black, 1969.

GARWOOD, G. T., *Gough Thomas's Second Gun Book*.

HARE, C. E., *The Language of Field Sports*, Country Life, 1949.

HARRISON, JEFFERY G., *A Wealth of Wildfowl*, Corgi, 1973.

JACKSON, W. A. (ed.), *The Complete Book of Gundogs in Britain*, Barrie & Jenkins, 1974.

JEFFRIES, RICHARD, *The Amateur Poacher*, Tideline, 1973 (facsimile of 1878 edition).

JEFFRIES, RICHARD, *The Gamekeeper at Home*, Tideline, 1973 (facsimile of 1879 edition).

JOHNSON, C. E., *The Game Laws Simplified*.

KEMP, MICHAEL, *A Shoot of Your Own*, Black, 1978.

MOXON, P. R. A., *Gundogs: Training and Field Trials*, Popular Dogs, 1973.

MOXON, P. R. A., *Gundogs: Modern Training Methods*.

PARKER, ERIC, *The Shooting Week-end Book*, Seeley Service.

PAYNE-GALLWEY, Sir R., *Shooting*, 2 vols., Badminton Library.

POWELL, BILL, *The Grey Geese Call.*

SEDGWICK, NOEL M., *The Gun on Saltings and Stubble*, Herbert Jenkins, 1949.

SEDGWICK, NOEL M., *Shooting round the Year.*

SEDGWICK, NOEL M., *Shooting Wildfowl and Game.*

SEDGWICK, NOEL M., *With Dog and Gun.*

SEDGWICK, NOEL M., *The Young Shot*, Black, 1975.

SEDGWICK, NOEL M., WHITAKER, PETER, and HARRISON, JEFFERY, *The New Wildfowler in the* 1970*s*, Barrie & Jenkins, 1979.

SHARPE, R., *Dog Training for Amateurs*, Country Life, 1955.

SHEPHARD, MICHAEL, *Come Wildfowling*, Museum Press.

STANBURY, PERCY, and CARLISLE, G. L., *Clay Pigeon Marksmanship*, Barrie & Jenkins.

STANDFIELD, F. G., *Syndicate Shooting.*

THOMAS, GOUGH, *Shotguns and Cartridges for Game and Clays*, Black, 1975.

Index